Foreword

Since 2000 the Chippenham Museum and Chippenham Town Council, has worked to the key aims of the Museum Service to work with, and promote, the heritage of Chippenham and area by raising the appreciation of our community heritage, tourism, town trails, exhibitions and publications.

In 2010 Chippenham Museum embarked on a new publication programme called Chippenham Studies in order to facilitate ongoing research based on both the Museum collections and the archives in the Wiltshire & Swindon Heritage Centre.

Further research on topics in Chippenham and the surrounding parishes has resulted in the need to extend the Chippenham's Studies publication into a new research series which allows local topics to be covered in much greater depth.

The first in the research series is 'Music, Organs and Composers of St Andrew's Parish Church, Chippenham' by Christopher Kent. This publication is a broadly based documentary and sociological study, which relates to the history of the Brice Seed organ of St. Andrew's Parish Church and also charts professional organists and composers, in particular the Coombs family.

This initial volume in the research series has been written and researched by Christopher Kent and allows the reader to follow different aspects of the history of music in St Andrew's Parish Church, Chippenham.

Melissa Barnett and Mike Stone
Joint Series Editors

Music, Organs & Composers

of St. Andrew's Parish Church Chippenham

Christopher Kent

Music, Organs and Composers of St. Andrew's Parish Church Chippenham.

A Documentary Study
by
Christopher Kent

Ph.D., M.Mus., F.R.C.O., F.S.A.
Hon. Fellow University of Reading.
Hon. Organist Bowood Chapel.

Cover illustrations:

Watercolour by William Davis looking West from the Chancel ca.1846
Canon Jackson Wiltshire Collection, courtesy of The Society of Antiquaries of London.
Photomontage of the 1752 Seede case as it would appear restored to a
new West gallery location as proposed in 2003.

Frontispiece:

A photomontage of the restoration as planned for the aborted
'St. Andrew's Project' of 2003-2005 (author and Paul Connell)

Dedication

To the memory of Thomas Wanless who first encouraged my interest in
Historical Musicology.

Preface to the Third Edition

It was the plethora of hearsay over the identity of the original builder of the present instrument that first prompted the archival research which led to the publication of the first edition of this work as a short documentary investigation in 1976, coinciding with the foundation of The British Institute of Organ Studies. This established unequivocally that the organ was initially the work of Brice Seede in 1752. The costs of printing and publication of this, and a second edition in 1984 which added further information, were generously met by the Vicar and Churchwardens whose constant encouragement of this work was still evident, and much appreciated by the author. Forty years later, many alterations have taken place within the building and to the organ. Changes of organists, clergy and churchwardens and financial pressures within the church have contributed to a decline of aesthetic sensibility and historically informed attitudes. The latter being somewhat at variance with the increased awareness of such cultural values in our society as a whole. Therefore, the time is appropriate for this extended and revised third edition for future generations including an overview of the present situation in the aftermath of the failure of the St. Andrew's project in 2005 (see Appendix XII). This is particularly pertinent in the light of the historically sensitive restorations of organs by Richard Seede at Lulworth Castle Chapel by William Drake (1986-1989), and recently, of the instrument by Brice Seede in the Music Room of Powderham Castle by Goetze & Gwynne (2012-2013).

Acknowledgements

The writer extends grateful thanks to the following individuals for their support and advice: Heather Ault, Mel Barnett, Alan Burgess, Ian Bell, James Berrow, Roger Robilliard, Relf Clark, Paul Connell, Paul Fortune, the late Brian Frith, Dominic Gwynn, John Harper, Catherine Hassell, Beth Hathaway, Richard Hird, Peter Horton, David Knight, Katie Manns, the late Rodney Matthews, Fiona Palmer, Andrew Prior, Jenifer Roberts, Michael Stone, Nicholas Thistlethwaite and Emma Whitcroft. Thanks are also due to the staff of the following institutions for their professional services: the Wiltshire and Swindon History Centre; the Chippenham Museum and Heritage Centre; the British Library: Departments of Rare Books, MSS & Newspapers; the Library of the Wiltshire Archaeological and Natural History Society, Devizes; the Libraries of the Royal College of Organists, the Royal College of Music; the British Organ Archive (University of Birmingham, Cadbury Research Library, Special Collections); The Library of The Society of Antiquaries of London; The Libraries of The Athenaeum, London; Lambeth Palace; the Royal Institute of British Architects; the National Archive; the National Portrait Gallery; the National Monuments Record; the Durham and Gloucestershire County Record Offices; the Victoria and Albert Museum (R.I.B.A. Archive) and the University of Reading, Department of Chemistry. Finally, my thanks to Chippenham Museum and Civic Society for supporting the publication of this work. Without the encouragement and patience of my wife Susan this work would not have been completed.

Christopher Kent,
Tytherton Lucas, July 2019

Abbreviations

L.B.L.	British Library, London.
B.I.O.S.	British Institute of Organ Studies.
B.O.A.	British Organ Archive.
C.B.S.	Church Building Society.
D.C.R.O.	Durham County Record Office.
G.R.O.	Gloucestershire County Record Office.
I.C.B.S.	Incorporated Church Building Society.
J.B.I.O.S.	Journal of the British Institute of Organ Studies.
L.P.L.	Lambeth Palace Library.
N.A.D.F.A.S.	National Association of Decorative and Fine Arts Societies.
N.P.O.R.	National Pipe Organ Register.
R.C.O.	Royal College of Organists.
R.C.M.	Royal College of Music
R.I.B.A.	Royal Institute of British Architects.
R.I.S.M.	Répertoire International des Sources Musicales, established in 1952 by the International Musicological Society and International Association of Music Libraries.
S.A.L.	Society of Antiquaries of London.
V.& A.	Victoria and Albert Museum.
W.H.M.	Wiltshire Heritage Museum, Devizes.
W.S.A.	Wiltshire and Swindon History Centre, Chippenham.

Contents

Appendices

Music Examples

Illustrations

The Sixteenth and Seventeenth Centuries

Plate 1: A stained glass representation of a Portative Organ in the East Window of the Beauchamp Chapel, St. Mary's Collegiate Church, Warwick. ('Images for Stained Glass' webs-site index).

The 250 year history of the present organ is not untypical of many instruments: changes to the building, habits of worship, music styles, alternative technologies and varying requirements of organists and clergy have brought the instrument to its current hybrid condition. It comprises work by quality organ builders of the eighteenth and nineteenth centuries and some by those of varying standards from the twentieth century. During the sixteenth century Protestant and Puritan hostility towards the use of organs in worship in both cathedrals and parish churches thrived amid the vicissitudes of the English Reformation during the short reign of Edward VI (1547-1553). For example: in 1552 Bishop Holgate of York had decreed 'that there be no more playing of the organs ' during services, and at Worcester Cathedral, Bishop Hooper ordered the dismantling of the three organs, which were duly reassembled at the accession of Queen Mary in1553. The research of Andrew Freeman cites numerous sales of organs through the 1560s, 70s and 80s, particularly in the City of London.[1] This also extended to Wiltshire, where in 1562 the church of St. Mary's Devizes sold 40 lbs. of 'organ pypes and the copper at 6d'.[2.5p.] per lb. for the sum of 20 shillings [£1], only to be followed by a new instrument two years later! [2]

The earliest extant record of an organ in Chippenham Parish Church, or of any musical activity, is contained in John Aubrey's Wiltshire Topographical Collections of A.D. 1659-1670:

'In the chancel on the North side is a very good organ loft of freestone carved......In the remembrance of the Sexton was an organ, the place where it stood is of good old free stone work. They say it was sold to Lacock.' [3]

There are many illustrations of positive or votive organs in drawings, paintings or stained glass as in the East Window of the Beauchamp Chapel in St. Mary's Warwick, restored after the Puritan damage of 1643 (Plate 1).

Buckler's painting of the north door of the chancel (Plate 2) shows the crenulations of what may possibly have been a return of the organ loft noted by Aubrey. On this slender evidence Aubrey continued to speculate that St. Andrew's might have been a collegiate church but Jackson questions this on the grounds that it was related to a Chantry Chapel dedicated to St. John the Baptist, now the site of the clergy vestry.

1

Daniell [4] described this North chapel as follows:

'*Outside the Chancel was a Norman buttress of extraordinary breadth supporting a fourteenth century staircase which certainly did not lead to a Rood Loft, as it would have obscured the two windows, but to a Minstrel's Gallery.*'

The same writer also cites references to nineteen Cantarists or Chantry Priests appointed by the Prior of Monkton Farleigh between 1333 and 1545.[5] However, at the Dissolution in 1536 the assets of this chapel were valued at 2s. 3d. for the altar cloths and vessels, and the endowment amounted to a value of £5 per year.[6] There was no mention of the organ reported by Aubrey.

Who may have constructed this small organ in Chippenham? As the Parish records are silent we can only speculate. Although stemming initially from South Molton, Devon, the Chappington family are possibilities, being within relatively easy access to essential supplies of fine Cornish tin they were active as organ builders through several generations from 1536 to 1620.[7] Their work extended throughout much of Southern England, and included in this area instruments in Bristol, Mere, Oxford, Salisbury and Winchester, of which no details other than accounts have been discovered. [8]

Plate 2: The North doorway of the Chancel with a possible remnant of the crenulated Chantry Chapel organ loft above.

Drawing by Buckler (courtesy W.H.M).

It is clear that the portion of carved facade (4' 10" x 1'7") which was set in the south wall of the sanctuary above the Sedalia during the 1875-1878 alterations (Plate 3) may have been one of the returns of the organ loft mentioned by Aubrey. His recounting that is was in memory of the Sexton may be questionable in view of Daniell's description of a fourteenth century chantry chapel mentioned above. It is unlikely to have accommodated more than a small portable votive organ. Such instruments were quite cramped in many English buildings [9] with between no more than a single keyboard with a compass of either forty notes from 5'F- a2 (or of forty-six notes CC-a2) with three to five stops.[10] The music played would have followed the Catholic liturgical tradition of plainsong performed 'in alternatim' with organ verses interspersed between those sung as unaccompanied chant. The nineteenth-century Churchwarden John Noyes also noted that Aubrey considered the stone to have been the facade of an organ gallery. [11]

Plate 3: The same fragment as set in the South wall of the Sanctuary above the Sedalia in 1878 (author).

If an organ had existed it would have fallen victim to the iconoclastic Commissioners who visited the parish following Edward VI's Act of Parliament of 1547, which contained prohibitions of images, more extreme than those of Henry VIII in 1538. After a period for voluntary compliance, there followed the wanton destructions of images, stained glass, rood lofts, organs, screens, chantry chapels, vestments and all other symbolic traditions that were similarly proscribed.

Following an interruption during the short reign of Queen Mary (1553-1558) the vernacular liturgy of the Act of Uniformity of 1549 returned with the first edition of the *Book of Common Prayer*. This was followed in 1550 by John Marbecke's *Booke of Common Praire Noted*, sung unaccompanied with or without the leadership of a Parish Clerk.

A further possibility arising from Aubrey's account that the instrument was 'sold to Lacock' may equally have been in response to the Parliamentary Ordinance of 1644 which called:

'for the speedy demolishing of all organ, images and all matters of superstitious monuments in all Cathedrals and Collegiate or Parish Churches and Chapels, throughout the kingdom of England and the Dominion of Wales, the better to accomplish the blessed reformations so happily begun and to remove offences and things illegal in the worship of God'

So was the 'votive' organ from a former chantry chapel in Chippenham Parish Church, mentioned by Aubrey, as being 'sold to Lacock' initially set up in the Abbey, and then moved into a loft in the chancel of Lacock church c.1632 as referred to in the Parish records? The possible hearsay of Aubrey may be supported by this reference in the records of Lacock Church of 20 June 1635:

An order of Dame Olliffe Stapleton widdow p[er]mitting of

A paire of staires in the Chancell to get upp to the Orgaines. [12]

3

Dame Olive Stapleton (d.1646) of Lacock Abbey was the patron of the village church, and her son Robert the incumbent. No trace of an organ loft survives today following the rebuilding of the chancel in 1777, but it is probable that the organ would have been removed or destroyed in the course of the Civil War. Lacock being the last Royalist stronghold in Wiltshire to be taken by Cromwell's army on 26th September 1645.

The records of the Wiltshire 'wool church' at Steeple Ashton also contain a similar reference to the seventeenth century demise of organs in parish churches, where an inventory of 1609 records the existence of 'certaine old pipes and fragments of the organ'. These were later sold in 1620 for 14s. 6d. [£69-60].[13] The Chippenham Church Account Book for the period 1620-1673[14] does not contain any references to the sale of an organ to support Aubrey's report. It contains an inventory of 'ornaments' in the church in 1620, but this does not mention musical instruments or music books. The books comprised: 'A Bible for the Clark's use references and / Two Common Prayer Books/ A Booke of hommyles/ Erasmus paraphras[es]/ A Booke of Marters [Foxe].' In 1627 the Apparator was paid 2 shillings and 8 pence for 'certaine new Books for the Church service.' A further Inventory of 1632 contains no references to anything musical, but there is an intriguing mention of the removal of gunpowder from the building during the Civil War.

During the Commonwealth, 2 shillings and 6 pence was paid to Edward Maundrell in 1651 'for defacing the King's Armes.' Presumably this followed Charles II's escape to France after his army was routed by Cromwell at the Battle of Worcester on the 3rd September. At his Restoration in 1660 a copy of the 'Booke of Common Prayer appoynted to be used ye 30 January' was purchased for 1 shilling and 4 pence. Subsequently the '[Ap]paritor' was paid 1shilling and 6 pence 'for ye prayer booke to be used on 29 May' being the King's Birthday.

Although the surviving parish accounts continue to make no references to music, it is not unreasonable to suggest that the unaccompanied singing of metrical psalms of the Reformation which met with the approval of the Cromwell's administration may have continued. After the first edition of Sternhold and Hopkins of c.1549, there followed John Day's *The Whole Book of Psalms*, the latter reappearing in successive editions between 1562 and 1687. Unaccompanied singing, invariably led the Parish Clerk with a pitch pipe became a cherished tradition in Parish churches which continued largely uninterrupted during the Civil War (Ex.1 Psalm 100). The Restoration may have been marked by the return of music led by choirs and organs in cathedrals, but it was far from being a similar watershed for parish churches particularly in rural towns. As Nicholas Temperley has commented: 'Writers on English music never tire of blaming the Puritans for everything that isn't as good as they would like it to be.'[15]

Ex.1: *The earliest printed edition of Psalm 100 (1560). (Harris Manchester College Oxford, Anglo-Genevan Collection).*

4

The Georgian Era

Following the Restoration and throughout the Georgian dynasty there was a gradual resurgence of organ building in provincial England. Stemming first from the largely professional music establishments of cathedrals and city churches, rural parish churches in key market towns gradually readmitted organs as acceptable adjuncts of their worship as the century unfolded. In mid-Wiltshire, the London organ builder Abraham Jordan junior (d.1756) provided instruments for Potterne Church in 1723[16] and for Calne Parish Church in 1729.[17] In the same year an organ was erected in Bradford-on-Avon church. Another London builder John Harris (d.1743) supplied an organ for Devizes Parish Church which was opened on 13 September 1743.[18]

Chippenham, as a '*rotten borough*' thriving on wool, cotton manufacture and agricultural produce, particularly cheese, was eventually to be no exception. However, until the middle of the eighteenth century it is possible that the only music in the worship at St. Andrew's would have been a continuation of the pre-Restoration unaccompanied singing of metrical psalms with each phrase 'lined out' by the Parish Clerk.

The next Churchwarden's Account Book of St Andrew's, for the period 1673-1733, is similarly devoid of any references to organs or instruments.[19] There is no documentary evidence (such as the purchase of bass viol strings for example) that could indicate there was even a gallery band of singers and instrumentalists. What might the standard of performance been like? The Remarks of William Hayes [20] in reply to Charles Avison's *Essay on Musical Expression*[21] give an unreservedly negative impression:

'*Our author has taken no small Pains, on the Article of Psalm-singing. He complains of a prevailing Method in performing Psalmody in our parochial service, which is that, of paying no regard to Time or Measure, and of drawling out every note to an unlimited Length;......I am inclined to think, that most congregations are apt to be guilty of dragging and singing too slow.'*

It was the persistence of this rhythmically ambiguous '*old way of singing*' that expedited introduction of organs to impose some musical order on the chaos. Hayes continued:

'*....it is in the Power of the Organist* (who he [Avison] *afterwards says ought to be the rational Guide and Director) in a great measure to prevent it.'* [22]

Canon William Lisle Bowles (1762-1850) expressed similar sentiments in his History of Bremhill in a chapter entitled 'Some Observations on Parochial Psalmody':

'*In country churches, singing to the 'praise and glory of God.'* in general, is little better than singing to the annoyance of all who have ear or heart for harmony. Two clarionets out of tune, and a bassoon which hurtles one note most sonorously, whilst three abortive blasts succeed, a man, for treble with long hair, and eyes out of his head: and a quavering bass, quavering for his life, and all those voices only agreeing on one point, as to which shall be heard the longest and loudest, such voices, and such instruments, not infrequently make up the musical part of country services, of the church service. An organ, though an humbler scale, unites the voices, and by the least the clergyman, unless entirely destitute of musical knowledge, may so regulate the manner of singing, that a common parochial- quior [sic], unless the members are very conceited, as ignorance usually is, may be drilled into something like cultivated and interesting singing.'[23]

As we are only too aware today, any form of change in worship, particularly in matters relating to organs can be a matter of vigorous debates and polemics. In the eighteenth century it was necessary for '*Music Sermons*' to be delivered [24] to justify the use of organs in divine services. These frequently fell back on arguments relating to 'antiquity' '*lawfulness*' and '*efficacy*'. As late as 1822 the Revd. John Eden in published his '… Sermon preached at the Opening of the New Organ in the Parish Church of St.Nicholas, Bristol, based on the words of Psalm 150 v.3. ('Praise Him with the sound of the trumpet: praise him with the psaltery and harp.) However, he added an opinionated and musically repressive handwritten note to his copy of the publication, expressing sentiments that may not yet have evaporated from some clerical minds of today:

'*One of the surest proofs of the good sense and right feeling of the Organist is the subdued and temperate use of his instrument, which he knows is intended, in accompaniments, to give and support, not to overpower the vocal part of the establishment….The enlightened Organist needs not to be told, that it is neither in the thunder or whirlwind of his instrument, but it is in its 'still small voice' that its influence will be experienced, the more immediate presence of the Deity be felt.*' [25]

Accounts of this period rarely record any financial or descriptive details and it often that the organs were donated by wealthy parishioners, patrons or syndicates. In Wiltshire, Potterne was an exception where the philanthropy of Mr. Thomas Flower supported from a fortune made from the West Indies sugar plantations. This included not only the gift of an organ, but also an endowment for the maintenance of the instrument and for an organist's salary which continues to this day. Although the vestry of Holy Trinity Church Bradford on Avon had agreed in 1729 that an organ be acquired with the necessary gallery built at the expense of the Parish, but the cost of the instrument was met by private donations and not installed until 1735.[26]

Eventually, in early January 1752 the documentary silence is broken in Chippenham through the minutes of an account of a Special Vestry Meeting held to discuss the gallery and seating alterations which would be required to accommodate an '*intended organ*.'

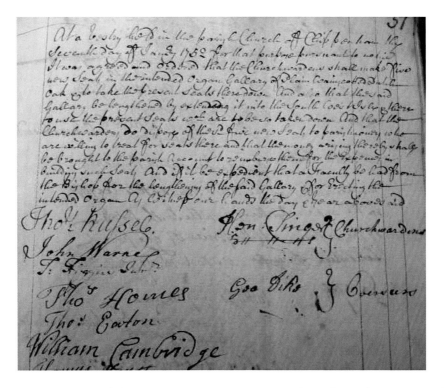

Plate 4. Minutes of the Vestry meeting concerning the gallery alterations and seating required to accommodate the Brice Seede organ (W.S.A.).

'At a Vestry held in the Parish Church of Chippenham the Seventh day of January 1752 for that purpose pursuant to notice. It was agreed and ordered that the Churchwardens shall make five new seats in the intended Organ Gallery of Plain Wainscotted Dutch Oak and to take the present seats there down. And also that the said Gallary be lengthened by extending it into the South West Isle and there to use the present Seats which are to be taken down. And that the Churchwardens do dispose of the said five new seats to parishioners who are willing to treat for seats there and that the money arising thereby shall be brought to the Parish Account to reimburse to reimburse them for the expense of building such seats. And if it be expedient that a Faculty be had from the Bishop for the lengthening of the said Gallary, and for erecting the intended Organ....' [27]

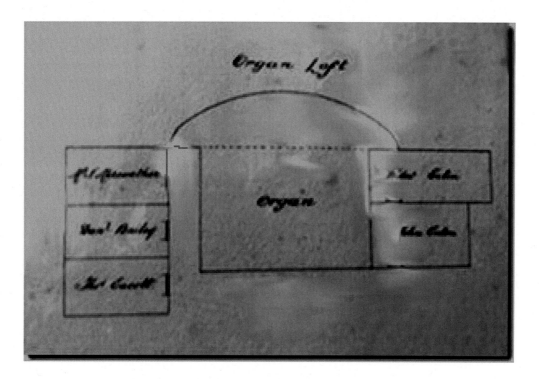

Plate 5: The Organ Gallery and adjacent seating from a plan of 1787.
(From a framed copy in St. Andrew's Church).

The faculty was presumably granted, but no copy has survived. The work of extending the gallery and installing the new seats was completed by the summer: the five sets were duly sold to parishioners at three guineas (ca. £270 in 2015) each on August 14th. [28] There is no documentary evidence as yet to suggest that the parish contributed to the cost of the organ. The only cost borne by the Churchwardens was three shillings (about £13 in 2015) paid to Mr Hite 'for the organ Curtins' on 10th August. [29] This may suggest that the building of the organ may have reached a fairly advanced stage. In the eighteenth century (unlike the nineteenth) the financing of what was to become the most expensive asset of the Parish, remains unclear. Who may have been among the donors? John Norris (c.1685-1752) of Nonesuch House, Bromham and The Ivy, an M.P. for Chippenham (1713-1715), and Anthony Guy, both former churchwardens, who had previously given two bells to the church in 1734? Norris died shortly after the Special Vestry Meeting and was buried on 11th January 1752 when Henry Singer (1708-1778) and Thomas Figgins (1703-1777) were the serving Churchwardens.

We might speculate that Norris, owner of The Ivy, and the donor of a bell in 1746, may also have been a posthumous benefactor, but his will has not been located. It may also be significant that the Freedom of the Borough was granted to the Vicar, the Revd. Christopher Holland, in

1752. Had he also made a personal contribution to the instrument? A scholar of Christ Church, Oxford from 1727 until 1738, when he was appointed to the living of St. Andrew's which he held until his death in office in 1760. He is interred in the Church. Equally, the Baynton family may also be considered as possible benefactors since the seating plan of 1789 shows that the family held a large pew in the Chancel.

It is this report of 1879 in the *Chippenham Chronicle* [30] that Churchwarden, John Noyes (printer and bookseller) provides the vital key to the early history of the organ:

'How the old organ at the parish church found its way there, and at whose cost it was erected, are questions which have afforded room for much speculation to the inhabitants of this town. The prevalent for many years was that the organ belonged to Salisbury Cathedral before the year 1780, when the splendid instrument which is now there was erected. This general opinion was, however, overthrown a few years back, when Mr. John Noyes discovered, nailed to a door in an empty house in High Street, a card, dated St. Cecilia's Day, [22nd] November 1752. This card was an invitation to a ball at the Angel Hotel in the evening. Mr. Noyes then made a thorough inspection of the organ and found upon it the following inscription 'John Eden, 1746.' These two different dates seem to imply that six years elapsed between the building and the opening of the organ - a thing not improbable.'

Unfortunately, there is a further lacuna in the church records for this date, but if we relate Noyes's information to *The Salisbury Journal* of 4th December 1752 [31] there is the following report:

'*On Wednesday last, being St. Cecilia's Day, was opened by Mr. Broadrip, organist of Bristol (at the head of a choice Band of Music), in the most solemn Manner, and before a crowded audience, the new Organ, built by Mr. Seed of Cirencester; when an excellent Sermon, preached by the Rev. Mr. Holland, demonstrated the Antiquity of Musical Instruments in the public Worship of God and recommended and enforced the Observance of that Duty in the most urgent and persuasive Manner. The organ was approved of as the compleatest and perfectest Thing of its kind by the best of Judges. In the Evening there were Balls at the White Hart and Angel Inns; and the whole thing was conducted with the greatest Decency and Harmony.*'

'Mr. Broadrip', one of a family of musicians active in the West Country through much of the eighteenth century, was likely to have been Edmund Broderip (1727-1779). He was one of many English pupils of the Italian violinist and theorist Francesco Geminiani (1687-1762) who had settled in London in 1711. In 1752 Broderip was organist of St James's, Bristol, and from 1764 of the Lord Mayor's Chapel. He also performed regularly at the Prince Street Assembly Rooms. He is possibly the Broderip later castigated by young Bristol poet Thomas Chatterton (1752-1770) in his satirical poem Kew Gardens:

This house of foolish cits and drunken boys
Offends my ears like Broderip's horrid noise. [32]

This organ is the first attributed to Brice Seede (1709/10-1790), a member of a Gloucestershire family[33] some of whose members were established in the crafts of joinery and wood carving. His name appears in the Churchwarden's Accounts of Cirencester Parish Church for the period 1750-1753 seemingly sharing the work of repairing the organ in association with Henry Millar of Gloucester.[34] Prior to this, Millar had announced in *The Gloucester Journal*[35] that he was moving from that city to his house:

'on Stoney Hill, near the Red Lodge, Bristol, where all Persons may be Supply'd with Instruments as Good as in London. He likewise repairs and tunes old ones...'

A further advertisement by Miller (apparently not a man to underestimate himself) which may have relevance to St Andrew's Chippenham appeared in the same news paper on 21 April 1752:

'To the PUBLIC Speedily will be finish'd An Entire NEW ORGAN for sale. Different from any in England being fit for either a Church or a Gentleman's Hall with a set and a half of Keys, the work so perfect as any in Europe having all the perfections the Number of STOPS can contain. For further particulars enquire of Henry Miller Organ Maker in Lewin's Mead Bristol...'

The short space of time in which the organ was built by Seede in Chippenham may reflect that the work was frequently shared between builders. The accounts of Cirencester referred to above show that both Miller and Seede received payments during the period 1750-1753 which cannot but support the possibility of their collaboration at Chippenham. Moreover the same source [36] records the payment of two shillings for 'A bottle of wine to ye Chippenham Organist.' This was possibly for Ben or James Millard who served from 1752-1770: payments to Ben Millard of 10s. 6d. per quarter were made during the period 1757 - 1759, and in 1758 seven shillings was disbursed on a coat for John Martyn the organ blower.

Of the possibility of organ builders collaborating on contracts in the eighteenth century Dominic Gwynn [37] has written as follows:

'I think your thoughts about the Chippenham organ are entirely possible. If Seede was not originally an organ builder, then one imagines he was like the elder Abraham Jordan – an organist/ organ nut who bought his way into organ building, supplying the capital to 'enable' projects, and employing unemployed locals. Jordan evidently employed ex-Smith people and learnt by copying the Smith organ at St George's Southwark. Seede may have done something similar with Miller, though Miller continued on his own account. The Powderham pipes are fairly characteristic – I haven't seen any quite like them before, so he may have learnt how to make them from someone in Bristol, and employed somebody to make them in Bristol... I would have been surprised by the speed with which they made organs then, but am not surprised now. When John Harris contracted to make the organ at St Thomas Bristol on 25.9.1728, he undertook to have it finished on 25.3.1729 (and was paid £200 on completion and £160 a year later! – perhaps these Georgian vestries drove a hard bargain). Either a number of workmen were involved, or much of it was from stock, or the contract was to some extent retrospective. But short lead–in times and short completion times were so usual in the contracts that survive, I think there must have been ways of meeting demand.'

However, this does leave open the possibility that the instrument may have had a previous location before being erected in Chippenham. The identity and provenance of John Eden remains a mystery, and no organ builder of the name has yet been identified from this period. It is also puzzling that in the 1870s Noyes did not observe Brice Seede's name above the keyboards as is customary. A possible explanation for this may be that it was lost when the console was altered during the interventions by Holdich at the centenary of the organ in 1852 (see below). Brice Seede acquired Miller's workshop at Lewins Mead Bristol in 1753[38] when the latter undertook work in the Midlands[39] and Liverpool[40] before settling in Dublin. [41] Seede continued to tune and repair his instrument in Chippenham: he was paid £3.15.6 for this service in 1757[42] and £5 in 1770 for 'Tuning and Repairing the Bellowes of the Organ as by Receipt.'[43] His son Richard (1743-1823) was paid two guineas for repairing and tuning in 1771 and four guineas in 1778.[44]

The Brice Seede Case

The facade of the 1752 case currently occupies the southern arch of the North Aisle organ chamber. It was recognized by the most aesthetically sensitive and highly cultured Vicar of recent times, Canon Philip Snow, as 'the greatest treasure of the church.' Furthermore, it is the sole surviving example of a characteristic West County case design of which the long destroyed examples at St. Mary Redcliffe, Bristol and St Andrew's Plymouth appear to have been the progenitors. Typified by three towers terminating with Corinthian capitals and constructed of oak. It was heavily stained and varnished during the nineteenth century but the original unstained and waxed finish is evident on the insides of the original console doors and in underside areas of the central pediment. Brice Seede's last case in this style which housed his instrument for the Parish Church of St. Petroc Bodmin (1775), presented to the Borough by the two Members of Parliament, has been totally destroyed. Fortunately, there is a water colour illustration in the Sperling Manuscript.[45]

Plate 6: The Brice Seede Case with its substantial crenulated pediment, was a particular feature of 18th century West Country organ cases. The Corinthian capitals of the outer towers are surmounted by angel trumpeters. Below are the poppy head finials of the flats. The inferior carving of the figure of St. Andrew mounted on the pediment suggests that it may have been added in 1879 (Roger Robilliard).

Plate 7: Angel with trumpet surmounting the Bass Tower (Roger Robilliard).

Note the untidy repair of the return of the central tower with softwood (top right).

Plate 8: a detail of the bass tower Corinthian capital (author).

Plate 9: The poppy head finial terminating the curved pipe shades of the North side flat (author).

Plate 10: The cherubim boss at the North end of the case terminating the elegantly carved frieze beneath the impost (author).

The three pipe fields of the large central tower are capped by the substantial pediment with inverted crenulations. Since these were photographed in 2005 by the present writer the short returns of these have disappeared. The semicircular outer towers are supported by brackets with cherubim bosses. Carved figures stand on each of the towers. Angels with gilded trumpets on flat caps of the outer towers angled towards a figure of St Andrew which surmounts the curved pediment of the central tower. As noted in Plate 5, there is a disparity in the quality of the carving: the fine quality of the Angels is not matched by the much rougher work of St. Andrew. This may suggest that the latter was an added when the instrument was moved in the nineteenth century.

As an elegant foil to the towers, the two intervening flats rest on square double panels, of which the inner portions are filled by delicately carved foliage. In 2007 the damage sustained to this during the twentieth century was restored by an anonymous benefactor. The pipe feet of the flats stand on straight toe boards and rise to semicircular pierced shades. These continue upwards with curved shoulders to terminate in poppy head finials.

Beneath the impost rails is a frieze decorated leaf decoration. Of the six panels beneath, the central pair formed the original console doors secured from within by a hand-forged bolt. The four outer panels are identical in size but for the one at the bass end. This is slightly wider with a keyhole suggesting that it was originally an interior access door.

The tide marks on the outer tower brackets and gaps beneath the panels of the flats would appear to indicate that the main structure of the case was moved slightly inwards when it was reassembled in the chamber. The façade pipes are non-speaking zinc dummies of 1879 on which can be seen the feint outlines of the diapering removed in 1965.

The rebuilding of 1879 also included lateral extensions to the original case to accommodate additional facade pipes. On the south side and above the doorway on the north side these comprise deal panels. The triangular pediment above the door may have originated from the balustrade of the original organ gallery. On the floor inside the organ are a number of timbers which may have formed some of the panels of the returns of the case when in the West Gallery. The dimensions are given in Appendices I and II. In 2013 two fragile drawings related to Gray & Davison's alterations were discovered as the lining of a Clergy Vestry chest drawer during the N.A.D.F.A.S. survey of the building. These show details of the above alterations but also give details of the raising of the case by some 15" on a new plinth, and show that before the existing door and pediment were inserted, possibly the original access door to the West Gallery, there was to have been a carved overhanging from the north end of the case above the passage behind the instrument.

In 2013 the writer found a fragment of the carved foliage on the floor inside the case, having been broken off during the 1987-1988 interventions. This was sent for laboratory analysis of the various layers of finishes, the results of this examination by Catherine Hassell are presented in Appendix XI.

* * *

James Morris Coombs 1

Few details have yet come to light of the career of the first organist of the eighteenth century: James Millard who was officially re-elected on 17th July 1753 after the completion of Seede's instrument. [46] With the appointment of James Morris Coombs (1769-1820) in September 1789 music in the church was in the professional hands of a former chorister of Salisbury Cathedral, trained as a composer and organist. [47] Coombs had also served an apprenticeship as a printer and his move to Chippenham was doubly fortuitous in that only six weeks after his arrival he married Elizabeth Forty, a widow, whose recently deceased husband had operated a printing business in the town.[48] A year later his first sacred composition, a setting of the *Te Deum and Jubilate* for the service of Matins in the Book of Common Prayer was published by Preston of London (Plate 11). It attracted an impressive subscription list of clergy, gentry, professional cathedral musicians, as well as those of provincial churches, notably the London composer and editor Dr. Samuel Arnold in addition to personal friends, pupils and local organists such as Henry Chiffence of Potterne.

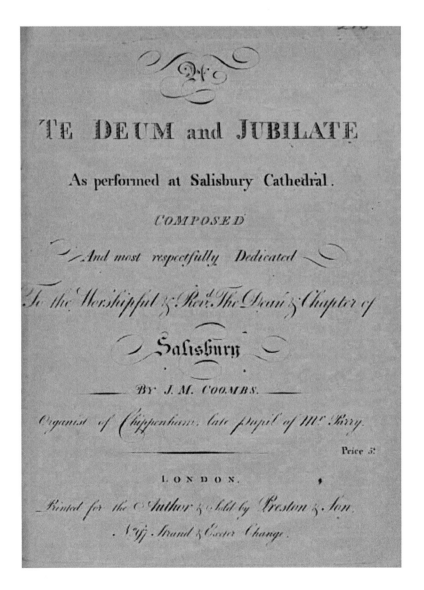

Plate: 11 title page of Te Deum and Jubilate set by James Morris Coombs I (1790).
(author's collection)

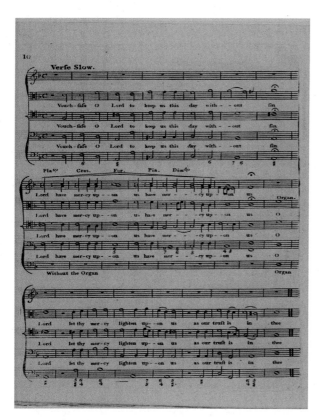

Ex.2 Coombs's Te Deum, in the mainly unaccompanied setting of verses 22-23, note the precise dynamic level abbreviations above the crescendo and diminuendo 'hairpins.' Also, harmonic details: a fleeting g sharp in the alto voice creates a deft Italian augmented sixth, and the doubled dissonances (9th& 7th) intensifying the expressive repetition of the word 'mercy.'

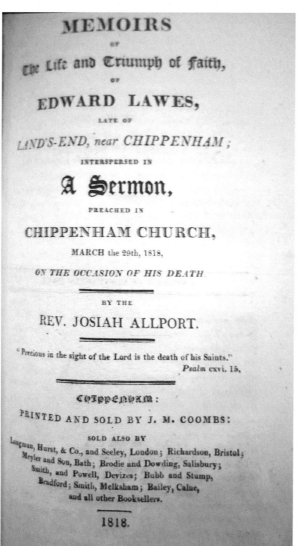

Plate 12: Coombs's publication of the Funeral Sermon delivered on the death of Edward Lawes (author).

As well as his printing craft, Coombs was also a bookseller in an advertisement of 1805[49] he is also named as a purveyor of 'Welshes female pills for the green sickness [anaemia] and other disorders incident in young females.' As the town's printer he produced posters and programmes, and towards the end of his life three sermons delivered at the Church by the incumbent and visiting clergy.[50]

15

In the aftermath of the Battle of Waterloo (1815) benefit services were held nationwide for the dependants of the fallen. Coombs directed music at those held at Bremhill and Chippenham:

'On Sunday the 20th instant a sermon was preached at the parish church of Bremhill....by the Rev. W.L.Bowles, and a collection made for the benefit of the widows and orphans of the brave men who fell at the battle of Waterloo. In the course of the service, which was conducted in a most devout and impressive manner, two pieces of beautiful music, with appropriate words from the pen of the Rev. Mr. Bowles, were sung under the direction of Mr. Coombs, of Chippenham, by several ladies and gentlemen present. One of these compositions, adapted to Dr. [Benjamin] Cooke's well-known glee. "How sleep the brave," containing the following eloquent stanza: -

"How sleep the brave, who sink to rest"
"By all their country's wishes blest!"
When cold upon the distant plain
The soldier lies mid heaps of slain,
We call on thee, O God, to bless
The Widowed and the fatherless.
Behold - behold the orphan's tear;
The sighs of mourning mothers hear;
And while, to soothe their bitter woe,
Compassion shall here write bestow,
Still let them kneel before thy throne,
And seek -- seek peace from Thee alone.

The church was overflowing; and the powerful arguments and truly pathetic eloquence of the preacher deeply affected the hearts of all present. A very liberal subscription followed on the occasion......a collection was made in Chippenham Church......amounting to £63 11s. 51/4d. [ca.£550 - 65p] after a most excellent sermon, preached by the Rev. Mr. Mogg."[51]

The London composer and organist of Westminster Abbey, Benjamin Cooke (1734-1793) originally composed this Dirge as a Glee in 1771 to words by William Collins (1721-1793) gaining the Prize Medal of The Glee Club. It was published in 1775[52] from which Bowles retains the first two lines. For the above performance, Bowles, or Coombs (presumably at the latter's request) substituted this text to Cooke's music. The incipit of which is shown in Ex. 3 below:

When cold upon the distant plain, The soldier lies mid heaps of slain, (Bowles)

Ex. 3: Benjamin Cooke's Glee performed as a Dirge partially adapted to words by Canon Bowles.

16

`For reasons of space, his secular compositions are largely beyond the ambit of the present study but their suave melodic elegance is reflected in his later church music A verse anthem 'Seek the Lord while He may be found'[53] (Isaiah 55, v.6) signed is ambiguously signed 'Co[o]mbs' is in 'Henry Baker's Book' a privately owned manuscript. This ambiguity does not exclude the possibility of it being the work of either of the William Coombes (1786-1850) or George Coombs (d.1769). James Morris Coombs included two tunes by George Coombs organist of Bristol Cathedral for the metrical Psalms 57 and 108 in his *Divine Amusement*. [54]

Ex.4: George? Co[o]mbs. Verse Anthem: 'Seek the Lord while he may be found' (private collection).

His *Divine Amusement of ca.*1819-1820 (Plate 11) was James Morris Coombs' only other publication of sacred music. This contains psalm and hymn tunes, an anthem adapted from Marcello as well as several of his original hymn tunes (Ex.5). A wide range of composers are represented including: Boyce, Handel, Haydn, Mozart, Pasielo, Pleyel, Tallis, and Charles Wesley. His neighbours are represented by the Broderips of Wells and Bristol. From Bath: Benjamin Milgrove (ca.1731- 1810), Precentor of The Countess of Huntingdon's Chapel, and Dr. Henry Harington (1727-1816) physician, composer, and one time Mayor of the City.

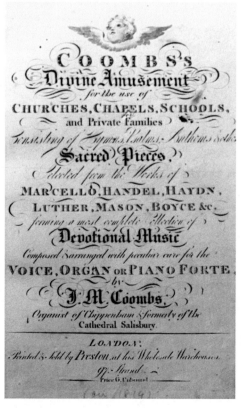

Plate 13: Title page of James Morris Coombs's 'Divine Amusement' (author's collection).

17

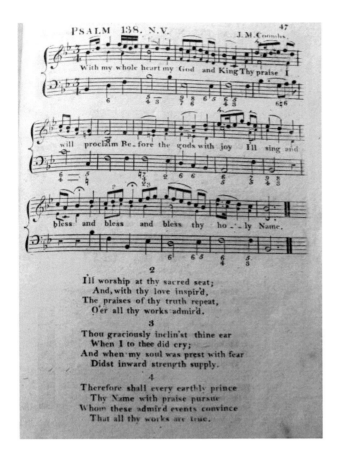

Ex.5: Coombs's Divine Amusement: an elegant melody for a metrical text of Psalm 138. (author's collectiion)

Ex.7: William Russell: Voluntary I (1804), second movement.

His repertoire of organ music included the first volume of Voluntaries (1804) by William Russell (1777-1813) in which his name and appointment appear in the list of subscribers. This also included local professional acquaintances including Messrs. Field and Windsor of the Abbey and St. Margaret's Chapel Bath respectively, and Corfe of Salisbury.

Distinguished London musicians include Thomas Attwood of St. Paul's, Dr. Charles Burney, Vincent Novello, Charles and Samuel Wesley, and the organists of several provincial Cathedrals.[55]

Coombs was a personal friend of the publisher, arranger and editor Vincent Novello (1781-1861). He was also acquainted with similar work by the Moravian minister, composer and editor Christian Ignatius Latrobe (1757-1836) who like Novello, edited continental Catholic music in vocal score often with an English text or translation. He also subscribed to a Harvest Anthem published in 1817 by George Gay (1771-1833) a self-taught quarryman musician of Monk's Chapel, Corsham. [56] Novello dedicated his arrangement of Mozart's Motet *Splendente te Deus* K.V. Anh. 121 to Coombs (Plate 14) which is a parody of the opening chorus of 'Thamos King of Egypt' K.V. 345 (Ex.6).

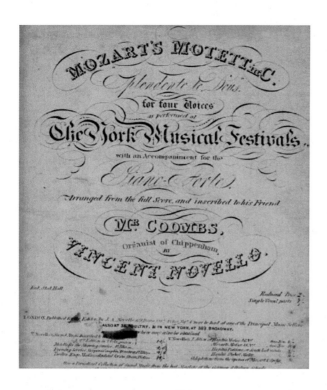

Plate 14: Vincent Novello's arrangement of Mozart's Splendente te Deus K.V. Ahn.121 inscribed to James Morris Coombs (author's collection).

Ex.7: Vincent Novello's arrangement of Mozart's Splendente te Deus for voices and organ inscribed to J.M.Coombs 1 (author's collection).

The Evening Service held on held on 28th February 1820, the funeral day of King George III included Alexander Pope's hymn 'Vital spark' as set by Edward Harwood (1707-1787) from Coombs's Divine Amusement (Ex.7).[57]

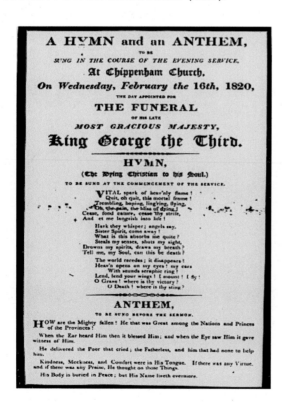

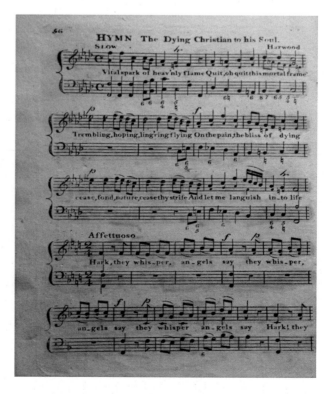

Plate 15: Evening Service for the Funeral day of King George III (Courtesy Wiltshire Heritage Museum)

Ex.8: Pope's hymn 'The dying Christian to his soul' to Harwood's tune (Coombs's Divine Amusement).

19

Perhaps through lack of space the poster does not name the composer of the Anthem: 'How are the mighty fallen....' The text draws together verses adapted from several scriptural contexts: 2 Samuel 1:25; Lamentations 1: Job 29:11-12; Ecclesiasticus 36:23; Philippians 4:8, and Ecclesiasticus 44:14. It is not inconceivable that the setting by the Salisbury Cathedral organist Michael Wise (1612-1687) was sung (Ex.8), which Coombs may have come to know from his early years there as a boy chorister. Moreover, its wide popularity is reflected in MS part books in some 40 sources, mainly located in Cathedral Archives.[58] It was transcribed into vocal score format by the Cambridge Professor Thomas Tudway (c.1656-1726) in a six volume anthology of Anglican Church music, some 3,000 pages, commissioned by Robert Harley, 1st Earl of Oxford.[59] However, there is also the possibility that Handel's setting (H.W.V. 603-4) of the same text for the Funeral of Queen Caroline may have been the work performed.

Ex.9: Michael Wise, 'How are the mighty fall'n.' (Lbl. Add. MS. 30932).

This service was among Coombs's last duties since he died on 8th March, one day before, (being High Bailiff), he was due to serve as Returning Officer for the Borough[60] and announce there return of two Members of Parliament following a General Election. His son, James Morris 11 contributed an article on his father for *Sainsbury's Dictionary of Musicians* which was repeated in the first edition of Brown and Strattton's *British Musical Biography* the full unedited text is given below.[61]

'James Morris Coombs was born at Salisbury – was admitted a Chorister in the Cathedral and received his musical education from Dr Stephens and Mr. Parry. – At an unusually early period of life, he composed and published a "Te Deum" which was much admired for its originality, which is still occasionally performed various Cathedral Churches - In 1789 he was appointed Organist of Chippenham – he afterwards published several single Songs, Glees, a Set of Canzonets & many of which were very popular. In 1819 he edited a Selection of Psalm Tunes which is very highly approved of, and has an extensive circulation – his last attempt in Composition was an "Agnus Dei" by competent judges deemed particularly beautiful- it has hitherto remained in Manuscript, but is now about to be published [no evidence of this has yet come to light]. He died in March 1820; Aged 52, & to the great grief of musicians and numerous friends who properly appreciated his great professional abilities, and who respected his social qualities as a neighbour.'[62]

His name is also included in some nineteenth century European reference sources: F.J.Fétis[63] and Hugo Reimann.[64] A short entry by Henry Hadow appeared in the first two editions of *Grove's Dictionary of Music and Musicians.*[65]

The Regency Period

In 1817 oil lighting was installed into the church, and the addition of pedals and other alterations to the organ, costing £51.4.0 (= £2,533.89) are discussed below. On 16th August 1819 the organ was tuned and repaired by James Butler,[66] an apprentice of George Pike England, whose new instruments in Wiltshire included those at Bishops Cannings and Warminster. On 7th July 1830 the instrument was tuned by [67] Fricker of Green Street, Bath.

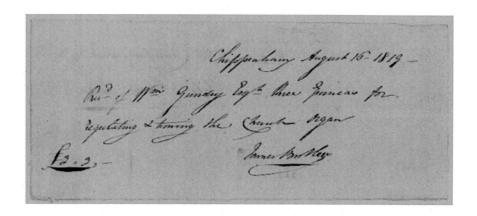

Plate 16: Tuning receipt of James Butler, August 16th 1819 (W.S A.).

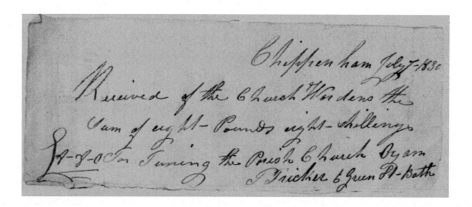

Plate 17: Tuning receipt of P. Fricker of Green Street, Bath, July 7th 1830 (W.S.A.).

Information from a mid- nineteenth century chronicler of organs is contained in the notebooks of the Revd. John Hanson Sperling (1825-1894),[68] who also attributed the organ to Brice Seede. Sperling worked on his collection of specifications between c.1850 and 1854 but there is evidence to suggest that he visited all of the instruments described in person. His specification for Chippenham is given below, albeit with the erroneous inverted date of 1725:

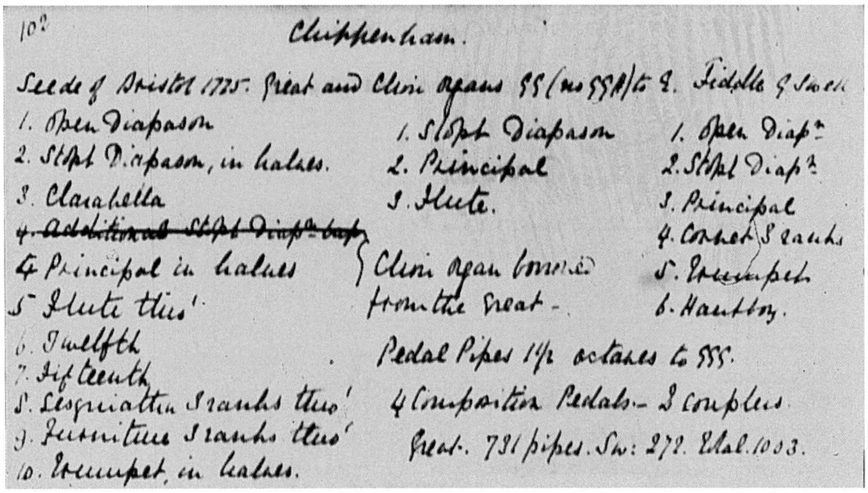

10?

Chippenham.

Seede of Bristol 1775. Great and Choir organs GG (no GG#) to E. Fiddle G Swell

1. Open Diapason
2. Stopt Diapason, in halves.
3. Clarabella
~~4. Additional Stopt Diapn bass~~
4 Principal in halves
5 Flute thro'
6. Twelfth
7. Fifteenth
8. Sesquialtra 3 ranks thro'
9. Furniture 3 ranks thro'
10. Trumpet, in halves.

1. Stopt Diapason
2. Principal
3. Flute.

Choir organ borrowed from the Great.

1. Open Diapn
2. Stopt Diapn
3. Principal
4. Cornet 3 ranks
5. Trumpet
6. Hautboy.

Pedal Pipes 1½ octaves to GGG.

4 Composition Pedals – 3 couplers.

Great. 731 pipes. Sw: 272. Total. 1003.

Plate 18: Sperling's specification of the organ after the 1852 alterations by Holdich. (Courtesy the Royal College of Organists).

The Sperling stop list given above does not give the instrument's original disposition on account of the presence of the Clarabella, the Pedal Keyboard, Composition Pedals and Couplers. Some of these could relate to the expenditure of £51.4.0. paid on 20th April 1830. It is probable that the Clarabella replaced a Mounted Cornet for which there is evidence of the location a separate wind chest or stage inside the case. The compass of the pedals and the Clarabella and composition pedals reflect the innovative work of J.C. Bishop (1783-1854) from around 1820. [69] The addition of pedal pipes would have implications for the winding, and it is likely that a double feeding bellows, or a double- rise reservoir with concussion valves, replaced Seede's original wedge bellows to ensure an adequate wind supply to the pedal pipes. New information has recently come to light that these alterations were the work of George Maydwell Holdich (1816-1896) in 1852.

James Morris Coombs II

James Morris Coombs II (1799-1873) succeeded his father as organist. He had clearly assimilated fluency as a player from his father, performing the *Concerto in Bb* of Paradies (1709-1790) as a 'middle voluntary' (Ex.10) during a service in aid of the Society for the Promotion of Christian Knowledge on 20th September 1820. The order of service (Plate 19) [70] which he also printed, gives details of the anthems performed by professional soloists from Bath. The service began with two excerpts from Handel's Messiah. The Psalms were followed by the above mentioned Paradies Organ Concerto as the 'Middle Voluntary, 'and the collects were followed by Maurice Greene's (1695-1755) anthem 'Acquaint thyself with God' (Ex.11) from his *'Forty Select Anthems'* (1743). The R.H. obbligato for the organ was ideally suited to the mounted Cornet stop that was displaced by the Clarabella in 1852.

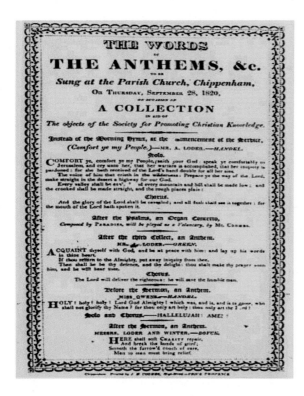

Plate 19: The service leaflet for the service in aid of the S.P.C.K. on 20th September 1820 (W.H.A).

Ex. 10: Paradies Concerto in Bb (Welker, London ca. 1768): Introduction and Allegro.

Ex.11: Maurice Greene 'Acquaint thyself with God.'

The music of 'Anthem before the Sermon': 'Holy, Holy…' is by Handel, but not the text. This is from Samuel Arnold's (1740-1802) pasticcio oratorio 'Redemption' (1814). It originated as the main section of the Bertarido's aria *Dove Sei amato bene* in Act I scene 6 of Handel's Opera Rodelinda (1715) HWV19. This, one of Handel's exceptionally beautiful melodies, was subsequently set to other texts: and it continues to be recycled today. Charles Burney (1726-1814), one of Britain's first great music historians described it as 'one of the finest pathetic airs that can be found in all his works.' The incipit of Arnold's arrangement is below (Ex.12). It also became

23

popular with organists as a 'Middle Voluntary' appearing in successive editions of 'The Organist's Companion' compiled by Sir John Goss (1800-1880).

The aria after the sermon: 'Here shall soft charity repair' by William Boyce (1711-1779) was from the anthem 'Blessed is he that considereth the poor' specially composed in 1755 for The Festival of the Sons of the Clergy in St.Paul's Cathedral. Scored for a quartet of male voices, it became very popular and published in a duet arrangement by Barnes and William Ayrton reported in *The Harmonicon* that 'the duet is as popular as ever, perhaps more so, for the music is 'better understood than formerly.'[72] Ex. 13 below.

Ex.12: Holy, Holy Lord God almighty. 'Redemption,' Arnold/Handel.

Ex.13: William Boyce: 'Here shall soft charity repair.'

24

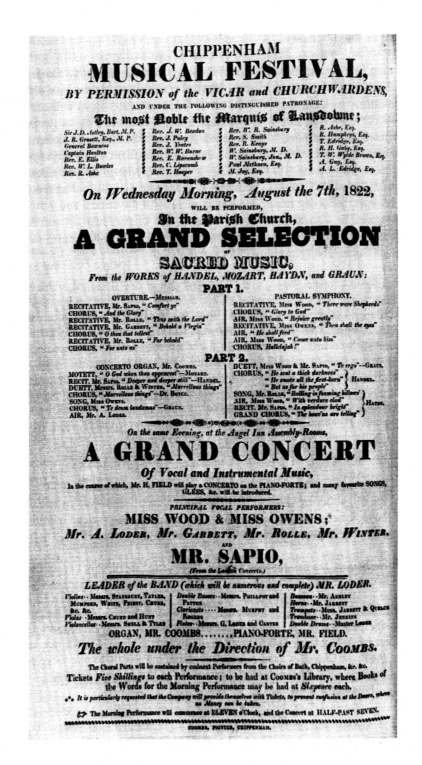

Plate 20: Chippenham Music Festival 1822 (courtesy W.H.C.)

On 7th August 1822 Coombs directed a one day music festival in Chippenham (Plate 20). The first part of the programme, a concert of Sacred Music in the Parish Church was built around well-known movements from Part One of *Messiah* before jumping abruptly to the 'Hallelujah Chorus' of Part Two.

The second part of the morning programme opened with an unnamed Organ Concerto. Although Coombs could have sourced Mozart's motet 'O God when thou appear'st (K.V. Anh.121) from Christian Ignatius Latrobe's 'Selection of Sacred Music' Volume II (1806), it is most probable that it was performed from the vocal score edition with a keyboard reduction published by Vincent Novello which was inscribed to his father. (See Plate 14 above).

Then followed by the dramatic tenor recitative: *'Deeper and deeper still'* from part II of Handel's oratorio *Jeptha* (H.W.V. 70). The duet and chorus *'Marvellous things'* is an extract from William Boyce's verse anthem *'The Heaven's Declare the Glory of God'* (1790). The opening chorus, an unidentified 'Air' and the duet *Te ergo* from Heinrich Graun's (1704- 1759) setting of *Te Deum*. The opening 'Grand Chorus' had previously been arranged for voices and organ by Coombs's father and published by Preston in 1815.[73] The morning programme concluded with three choruses Handel's oratorio 'Israel in Egypt' and three arias and the chorus *'The Heavens are telling'* from Haydn's 'Creation.'

The evening concert featured the tenor Antonio Sapio (1792-1851) born in London, trained by his Italian father he was fresh from his debut earlier that year. His engagement by Coombs was the first of many provincial performances that extended to Festivals in York and Edinburgh.

The most distinguished piano pupil of Coombs senior was Henry Ibbot Field (1797-1848), son of Thomas Field (1776-1848) organist of Bath Abbey (1795-1832). Field had also made his London début earlier in 1822 giving the British premiére of Hummel's *Piano Concerto in A minor* Op.85 at a concert of the Philharmonic Society on 23rd February.

This event received an extensive review in *Keene's Bath Chronicle*:[74]

"Chippenham Musical Festival

Took place on Wednesday last; and it affords us much pleasure to be able to state that the attendance at the Church in the morning, and at the Concert Room in the evening, was numerous and respectable, even beyond anticipation. There was not a family of distinction within many miles of the town that was absent on the occasion; and the performances were altogether worthy of such distinguished patronage - they were so complete in every department , as, not only to afford subject of high commendation, in the present instance, but also to lay a most honourable for similar musical treats in succeeding years.

The Selection at the Church comprised the choicest pieces from some of the best Masters of Sacred Minstrelsy - the first part consisting wholly of extracts from the inspired Messiah, the sublime opening of which was given by Mr. SAPIO, in admirable voice, and with genuine expression. The fine recitative *"Thus saith the Lord of Hosts."* called forth the best powers of Mr. ROLLE, who displayed an energy and firmness, combined with neatness of execution, rarely to be met within bass voices. Mr. GARRETT, in *"Behold a Virgin,"* convinced his auditors that he has not, in the present day, his superior counter tenor for an oratorio. Miss WOOD was in excellent voice, and all her songs imparted that exquisite taste, refined judgement, and impressive melody, which are so unequivocally acknowledged in the musical circles of this city. - The recitative *"Then shall the eyes of the Blind,"* and the subsequent air, *"He shall feed his flock,"* are well suited to the sweet, soft voice of Miss Owen who as she gained confidence, gained favour with her auditors.

The Second Part commenced with an Organ Concerto admirably performed by Mr.Coombs; and was followed by a most judicious selection of Sacred Pieces - among which, SAPIO'S *"Deeper and deeper still,"* was conspicuously grand. Mr. A.LODER, gave a song by Geminiani, with his accustomed richness of tone, and well cultivated taste. The amateur must feel obliged to Mr. A. Loder , for his frequent introduction of new songs. - Mr. WINTER'S powerful voice was heard with admirable effect in a duet with Mr. ROLLE. The choruses went off with fine simultaneous grandeur; and evinced not only consummate skill in the performers, but also the great attention that must have been paid to this department by the director of the festival.

The Concert Room; in the evening, was crowded to excess. We do not have space to state the various pieces, but feel imperiously called on to notice Mr. H. FIELD'S Fantasia on the Piano-forte, in which he introduced the popular air of *"We're a'noddin,"* electrified the audience by the brilliance of his execution. We were also happy to observe, that his much esteemed father afforded his eminent assistance by presiding at the piano-forte with his well known masterly precision and commanding effect. We conclude with our hearty congratulations to Mr. Coombs, on the result of this, his first essay, as Concert Director - must be considered as a testimony of the high esteem in which his private as well as professional character stands among the nobility and gentry, of that highly respectable neighbourhood.

"Among the performers" says as correspondent "were several gentlemen from Corsham, Box &c. whose execution was highly creditable to their talents; and proves that the *Corsham Amateur Concert* is not only a rational and delightful amusement, but productive of other benefits to society, as it introduces into our orchestras those who feel pleasure in participation; and who, from mingling with professors of eminence, become competent judges of the art, and liberal supporters of the science in general, as is already evinced by several of the old members, whom we has the pleasure to recognise, as we do when any meeting takes place for the display of good music in this neighbourhood."

The frequent interaction between musicians of Chippenham and Bath had previously been established by Coombs's the elder, whose daughter as an accomplished soprano had made her Bath début at a benefit concert for William Herschel in May 1816 is described in *The Bath Chronicle as:*' handsome in person & unaffected in manner. [H]er voice is rich and flexible, and of extensive compass; her songs were executed in a finished style and were warmly applauded.'[75] The leader of the band Mr. John David Loder (1788-1846) for the 1822 Chippenham Festival was the most distinguished member of a dynasty of Bath musicians, a child prodigy performing a concerto and making his London debut at the age of 8. He rose to become leader of the Theatre Royal Orchestra in 1807, and 1817 was regularly engaged to lead the orchestras of the Philharmonic Society of London and the Three Choirs Festival. His career ended in London where from 1840 he was a violin professor at the Royal Academy of Music. Among Coombs's other Bath colleagues was James W. Windsor (1776-1853) organist of Margaret Street Chapel, for whom he made transcriptions of anthems by Blow, Croft and Humfrey as a gift in 1835.[76]

The friendship between James Morris Coombs senior and Vincent Novello continued through his son who requested that Novello scored his father's unpublished song[77] the text is from an anonymous serialised novel in *The Ladies' Monthly Museum or polite repository:* 'I like to behold the bright stream' expressly composed for this 1822 Chippenham concert. [78] This scoring was within the resources of the Festival Band: 2 flutes, 2 bassoons, 2 horns, and strings (Ex. 15)[79]

Ex.14 holograph of J.M.Coombs's 'I like to be by the bright stream.' (Royal College of Music)

28

I like to behold the bright stream.

W.L. Bowles (?)   J.M. Coombs

Ex. 15 The introduction as scored by Vincent Novello (B.L. Add. MS. 65489 ff.108-109v.)

A Bowood Interlude

From Plate 20 (above) and from the Journal of a Mary Berry (see below) it is evident that The Third Marquis of Lansdowne (1789-1863) [80] was a devotee of music heading the Patrons of the 1822 Chippenham Festival. In the following year the Private Chapel and Library were under construction at Bowood House to the classically inspired designs of Charles Robert Cockerell (1788 – 1863). A sketch of the proposed Chapel interior includes an organ case.[81] Cockerell had agreed on the provision of a recessed plinth for the Bowood organ with Lord Lansdowne on 29th January 1822[82] and his drawing for the organ case ['frame'] (Plate 21) was approved on 29th March 1823.[83] Cockerell chose to engage the London organ builder in Henry Bryceson (1796-1870) who modified his case design.[84] The curved pipe field and domed copula were not unlike the organ case designed by Cockerell for St. George's Hall Liverpool in 1851.[85]

Plate 21: Bowood Chapel as initially envisaged by Cockerell (Bowood Archives)

The Chapel was dedicated by the Revd. William Lisle Bowles on 21st December 1823. The writer Moore reported in the *Gentleman's Magazine* of 21st January 1824 that his sermon was 'much too long and desultory'. Coombs was appointed organist, and published an anthology of music for use in Chippenham Parish Church where he had succeeded his father as organist[86] (Plates 21-22 and Examples 15-16). This collection also includes compositions of his father and of the Bath composers William Linley (1767-1835) and the Abbey organist Thomas Field. (1776-1831). Coombs's duties at Bowood and the Chapel music are described in the Journals of Mary Berry who was a guest at the house in 1838:[87]

'Saturday 27th October....Since the two Liddells have been here[:] Lady Barrington and Lady Williamson we have had delightful music, and much of it, every evening. Their voices are admirable, although they have seldom sung any of my favourites. This morning we have been in the chapel, which very conveniently opens from the greenhouse. The organist of t/he neighbouring town comes every Saturday to instruct the parish children in singing. Our two ladies gave us several pieces of Handel divinely well, with the accompaniment of the organ; Lord Lansdowne always much enjoying music.' It is not certain whether the Cockerell - Bryceson case was replaced when the new organ was built by Holdich in 1843. No complete details of his instrument have yet been found, only the following report which appeared in *The Devizes and Wiltshire Gazette* of '16th November:

'A fine toned organ was opened on Sunday last in the Marquess of Lansdowne's private chapel at Bowood, by Mr. G.M. Holdich of London the builder. Mr. Holdich's newly invented improvement called the "Diocton" is introduced, and the instrument is altogether is altogether worthy of the beautiful place of worship in which it is erected.'

In 1899 it was replaced by an organ from the London home of Lord Revelstoke for whom it was built in 1886. By the mid-twentieth century this had deteriorated and the case was emptied of its components some of which were recycled elsewhere.[88] The case lay empty until it served to accommodate the present instrument built by Peter Collins in 2002 (Plate 23). On the advice of the present writer this was designed to replicate the tonal style of J.S.Bach's esteemed organ builder Tobias Heinrich Gottfried Trost (ca. 1679-1759). It follows many technical details from the small instrument of 1717 by the same builder in the *Walpurgiskirche* at Grossengottern, Thuringia,[89] which was restored by Eule of Bautzen in 1997.[90]

Manual I

Principal	8
Gedackt (wood basses)	8
Viol di Gamba	8
Octave	4
Quint	3
Superoctave	2
Terz	1 3/5

Manual II

Rohrflote (basses 1-24 from Gedackt)	8
Viol di Gamba (from Manual 1)	8
Spitzflote (basses from Octave 4)	4
Couplers	
Manual I to Pedal	
Manual II to Pedal	
Tremulant to whole instrument.	

Compass

Manuals CC-f3
Pedals CC-f1
Wind Pressure 72mm. throughout.
Suspended mechanical actions to manuals.
Mechanical actions to pedals and drawstops.
Tuning to Werckmeister III.

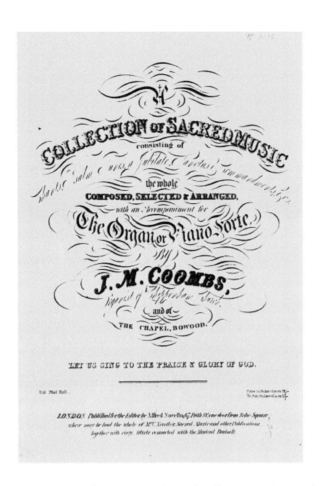

Plate 21: Title page of J.M. Coombs II 'Collection of Sacred Music.'

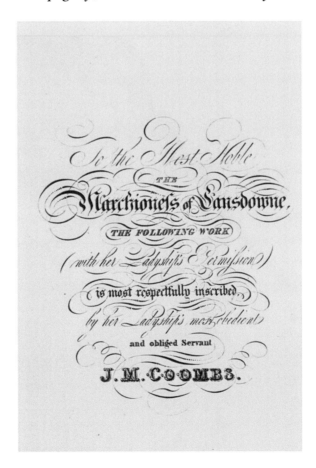

Plate 22: Dedication pages of J.M. Coombs II 'Collection of Sacred Music.'

Coombs's Collection comprises: 51 chants for four voices by Coombs, Field, Forster, Hoyle, O Linley, Wm. Linley, Mullins, Sainsbury and Windsor; 38 settings of metrical Psalms: 16 of his own, 3 by his friend J.W.Windsor (Margaret St.Chapel Bath), 3 by William Linley (Bath); 2 by the Revd. Ozias Linley; 2 by Dr. Sainsbury; 1 by the Revd.G. Mullins; 3 by Winter; 2 by Vincent Novello, whose harmonization of the 'Portuguese Hymn' (familiar as *Adeste Fidelis*) is the only hymn. Then follow movements from a Service Setting in G by Coombs *(Sanctus, Kyrie, Magnificat, Nunc Dimittis and Jubilate)* and finally his own Verse Anthem: 'Give ear unto my prayer.'

Ex. 16: J.M. Coombs II Sanctus.

Example 17: J.M. Coombs II Chants in D and d.

Example 17: J.M. Coombs II Chants in D and d.

33

Plate 23: The Collins - Trost Organ of 2002 in the Revelstoke case.

✳✳✳

𝔈arly 𝔑ineteenth 𝔆entury 𝔄lterations to 𝔆hippenham 𝔓arish 𝔆hurch.

Returning to St. Andrew's Chippenham, every generation has left its mark on this building. Continuing from the beginning of the 19th century with the late Georgian and Regency periods we would still find the Georgian furnishings: box pews, communion table, a central pulpit, galleries over the southern chapel (now the Baptistery), and in a place of honour, in the West Gallery, the greatest material treasure of the church: the organ built by Brice Seede in 1752. After a little more than fifty years its beauty and elegance were partially obscured by the plaster ceiling as can be seen in the frontispiece. This was to be the beginning of a syndrome of aesthetic insensitivity by successive church officials towards the finest surviving Baroque organ case in the West of England. On 25th June 1803 a contract was signed by Matthew Humphreys (Churchwarden) of Ivy House, and Anthony Guy (representing the Feofees) for the rebuilding of the church roof and the addition of a flat plaster ceiling, supported by slim cast iron columns, which obscured the upper details of the organ case. This was to the design and work of William Fellows, Surveyor of Southwark and the Builder William Patch of Finsbury Square, London.

Until recently, the only extant interior illustrations of this period are the rough watercolour sketches by William Davis of 1846 in the Jackson Collection in the library of The Society of Antiquaries of London (Plates 24 & 25). Jackson noted they were: 'a strange interior, as to perspective.' However, Jackson was not aware of Davis's finished paintings from the same sketches which have recently surfaced in the Goddard deposit in the library of the Wiltshire Archaeological and Natural History Society,[91] In the following year Sir Stephen Glynne in his 'Notes on Wiltshire Churches' described the interior thus: 'There is a modern ceiling, sadly low, and very large organ in the west gallery, to admit which it has been necessary to make an opening in the ceiling.'[92] It is also likely that Glynne would also have noted that this ceiling was acoustically detrimental to the building.

Plate 24: Interior sketch by Davis ca.1846 looking Eastwards (Society of Antiquaries).

Plate 25: Interior Water Colour by Davis ca.1846 looking Northwards (Society of Antiquaries).

35

Why were these 1846 drawings and paintings made? The vestry minutes may contain an answer: a reordering was essential to provide additional seating for the Poorer Parishioners. This was likely to have been a dilatory response to the Great Reform Bill of 1831 which established free seating in churches and the decline of pews rented only by Freeholders of the Parish. The vestry minutes also note that 'the seats to the east of the minister faced the west, those to the west faced east, but those to the south faced divers ways.'

The Oxford Movement

Although the Oxford Movement is usually considered to have been sparked by John Keble's sermon in the University Church of July 1833 in response to the Reform Act of 1832, it was followed by a tirade of pamphlets defending the doctrines of Apostolic Succession and the *Book of Common Prayer*. Inevitably the latter, and the advocacy of Catholic ceremonial traditions, courted opposition from Liberals and Evangelicals and also provoked opposition from the government and grassroots, while the provincial press was flooded with polemics between the Ritualist and Protestant factions of the Anglican Church. Led by the intellectual and spiritual strength of figures of the stature of John Henry Newman (1801-1890). On his defection to the Roman Catholic church a similar movement was associated by the distinguished Cambridge Hebraist and Ecclesiologist Edward Bouverie Pusey (1800-1882). The ripples of this Romantic return to the pre-Reformation roots of Christian worship and liturgies were to have significant consequences for the music traditions of many parish churches. It was a decade later before the full influence of this revolution and consequences for organs and choirs were felt in Chippenham. Yet in 1833, during the incumbency of the Revd. Lewis Purbrick (1815-1860): the box pews were removed, the floor partly repaved, the pay table discarded, the font moved from the south chapel to a more apt position by the west door beneath the organ gallery, and new open access pews installed. The cost of £893.2s.6d. [£52,274.61] was met largely by The Feofees of the Chippenham Church Lands, and donations from Christ Church Oxford, the Borough, local gentry, professionals, traders, and members of the congregation. An enquiry was sent to the Incorporated Church Building Society[93] regarding a grant, but this was not required.

The employment of Mr. Fisher, a gas fitter in 1833 indicates the end of oil lamps. The Borough Council minutes record that on 7 August Mr. Bowsher be instructed to remove the Corporation Pew 'until a proper and suitable pew is provided. 'On 25 August local architect John Darley was instructed to 'prepare a plan of the intended pew.'

In 1847 G. Alexander, the church's architect, approached the leading London organ builder William Hill (1789-1870) requesting an estimate for moving the organ from the west gallery to the Baynton Chapel in respect of which he wrote to Purbrick as follows: [94]

30 Bedford Square, London
May 8th 1847

Dear Sir,
I enclose your working Plans and Specifications for the Builders to estimate for the Church at Chippenham. I have kept as separate specifications the pewing works proposed to be done in the first instance, and those things desirable in the want of funds being provided I have written to Mr. Hill Organ Builder to know the cost of moving the organ from the West Gallery to the Baynton Chapel including tuning the same and he informs me it will be about £30 if in town and a trifle more in the Country.

A copy of his letter I subjoin. I believe you are aware that the Tower will accommodate rather more persons than the present Organ Gallery, and that therefore there will be no loss of accommodation by the removal, and as the effect of the Church will be much improved by the additional length of about 30 feet. I hope this will be found possible to accomplish. Should the Builders have any questions to ask relative to the estimates, it will be best to refer them to me. / I am Dear Sir,

Yours truly,

G. Alexander

William Hill replied to Alexander by return:[95]

Copy
12 Tottenham Court Road
May 8th. 1847

Dear Sir,
In reply to yours I beg to state that the probable expense of removing the organ you mention and erecting it tuned at the other end of the church would be if in London about £30. If in the entry the expense would be a trifle more.

I remain Dr. Sir/ Yours Obediently/ signed Willm. Hill.
G Alexander Esqre.

The renewal of the pews was completed and the relocation of the organ shelved. A second attempt was made to accomplish this five years later. Although the St Andrew's Vestry minutes [96] exist for the period 1829-1856, they are in a very fragile condition. Some typescript extracts made by Platts exist in the library in the Wiltshire Heritage Museum (Devizes) which contain the following entries:[97]

St. Andrew's Chippenham: Vestry Minutes 7th May 1852:

'A resolution was passed that the Organ in the Parish Church be removed from the gallery to the Chapel at the East end of the Church and that the gallery be put into a proper state of repair for the accommodation of parishioners provided no Church Rate be granted for that purpose.'[98] Not surprisingly, this provoked opposition as recorded in the ensuing vestry minutes of 20th July, (just as in 2005 the excellent plan to reinstate the organ from the Chancel to a new West Gallery was also to encounter resistance q.v. Appendix XII) :

'On the representation of the Organist and parties assisting in the Choir that the removal of the Organ to the Chapel at the East end of the Church would be [an] unsatisfactory arrangement the Vestry rescinded the resolution passed of the 7th May last, and that the Churchwardens undertake the repair of the Gallery.'[99]

An examination of the original water damaged document by the present writer revealed further information not included in Platt's transcription of the meeting:

'It having been represented by the Organist and parties assisting in the choir that the proposed removal of the Organ to the Chapel at the East End of the Church would be an unsatisfactory arrangement and not so desirable for the Organ as regarded the sittings of the whole Church the Vestry determined to rescind the resolution passed the seventh of May last and to continue [with] the Organ in its present position. It was proposed by Mr. W.H. Brinkworth and seconded by Mr. John Noyes.

It having been ascertained that the repair of the Gallery was necessary before the repair of the organ could be undertaken and an estimate having been submitted to the Vestry for such repairs amounting to £60.12.0 [£4,500] it was resolved that the Churchwardens should undertake the repair of the Gallery to that amount and should make an application to the Church Feofees for a grant in aid of the sum required. James Noyes. Chairman.'

This work was immediately put in hand and *The Devizes and Wiltshire Gazette* of 14th October 1852 published the following but not altogether accurate report:

'CHIPPENHAM. -- The organ of the parish church was reopened on Sunday last, after extensive reparations and additions, which have been ably executed by Mr. Holdich, of London. --- This fine old organ was erected, with those in Bristol Cathedral and St. Mary Redcliff[e], in the early part of the last century by Seed of Bristol [sic] Bristol Cathedral dates from 1685 and was the work of Renatus Harris and the organ of St .Mary Redcliffe that of Harris & Byfield in 1726 : the diapasons are especially remarkable for their richness and ful[l]lness of tone, and the chorus stops for their brilliance, the reed stops of the swell organ are also of great beauty and delicacy. It has 24 stops, 3 rows of keys, 11/2 octave[s] of German pedals with pedal pipes, and 4 composition pedals. By means of the mechanism now introduced, the performer is enabled to make 241 [sic] pipes speak at once, it is one of the finest instruments in the West of England. The musical services were, morning "*Venite*," chant Bellamy, "*Te Deum*" and "*Jubilate*" Tilleard in A, "*Sanctus*" Buck in A, the anthem *"Arise O Lord"* Rev. W.H. Havergal evening, chant Dr. Chard, *"Magnificat and Nunc Dimittis"* Boardman in G , the anthem *"Hold not thy tongue."* [John Cubitt] Pring. Mr. Coombs presided at the organ.'

The engagement of Holdich to carry out this work is not surprising in that James Morris Coombs II would have been familiar with his instruments in Bowood House Chapel (1843) and Calne Parish Church (1842).[100] This report also gives a good overview of the early Victorian repertoire of St. Andrew's choir. The details of the composers represented include:

The Revd. W.H. Havergal (1792-1870) whose anthem 'Arise O Lord' (Psalm 132 vv.8-9) was drawn from *The Lyra Ecclesiastica*[101] mainly homophonic and limited in harmonic resource it is grammatically correct and reflective of the composer's rejection of the melodic gaieties of the music of the pre-Victorian age. The organ accompaniment clearly reflects the newly acquired composition pedals in the changes to and from Full Organ (Ex.18). Today, Havergal is best remembered for his adaptations of hymn tunes including 'Christ whose glory fills the sky' and 'Blest are the pure in heart.'

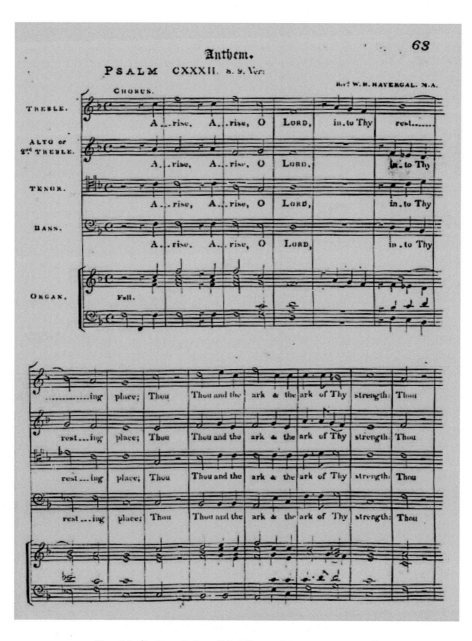

Ex. 18: 'Arise, O Lord' William Henry Havergal.

39

John George Boardman (1819-1898) published Sacred Music, a collection of psalm and hymn tunes in London, in 1844. A copy of his undated 'Evening Service' in G is bound into a volume owned by Sir George Grove in the library of The Royal College of Music.[102] Here it is only in his setting of *Nunc Dimittis* that the text induces a greater level of harmonic invention (Ex. 19).

Ex. 19: James George Boardman, Nunc Dimittis.

The evensong anthem by Jacob Cubitt Pring (1771-1799) is a setting of Psalm 83 from his 8 Anthems (1792). This setting of the late Georgian period demonstrates a fluency in independent part writing and fugal interest (Ex.20). [103]

Ex. 20: Jacob Cubitt Pring, Psalm 83.

The other composers represented mainly for their chants included: Richard Bellamy (1743-1813) who held posts as a singer and choirmaster at Westminster Abbey and St. Paul's Cathedral; James Tilliard (1827-1870) who compiled 'Collection of Sacred Music for Schools, in 1849; Dr. Zechariah Buck (1798-1879) organist of Norwich Cathedral, composer of anthems and chants, and Dr. George William Chard (1765-1849) organist of Winchester Cathedral, composer of anthems, services and chants.

At this point we might also consider what was happening to this church during the nineteenth century in a wider national context. It was a period unparalleled in church building since the Norman Conquest. By 1858, 9,000 new churches had been built in a space of 50 years to accommodate a doubling of the population. The 1851 census records that on Sunday 30th March: 7,261,032 out of the entire population of 17, 927,609 attended a church, and of these 52% were Anglicans. How does Chippenham's population compare with this? In 1801 the population stood at 3,336, but by 1891 it had grown to 5,392.

In the wake of these figures it is not surprising that the Victorian era also saw the meteoric rise in secular music making which was to continue to reach its zenith in the works of Elgar, Parry and Stanford before the decline inflicted by the Great War. The Chippenham Harmonic Society was founded in 1838, in 1854 *The Musical Times*[104] reported that at the conclusion of their sixteenth season they were presented with the complete works of Sir Henry Bishop (1786-1855) by Joseph Neeld M.P. for the Borough and the works of Dr. John Wall Calcott (1766-1821) by Milsom and son of Bath. 1858 saw the foundation of the Chippenham Choral Association; their second concert in the Town Hall on 26th April 1859, a choir of fifty under the direction of Mr. Samuel Gee drew a large attendance.[105]

The Revd. Canon John Rich

The eldest son of a clergyman, Rich was born at Ivinghoe, Buckinghamshire, educated at Westminster School, as Head Boy he was present at the Coronation of Queen Victoria, and entered Christ Church Oxford in 1844. He graduated B.A. in 1848, and was ordained Deacon in Oxford in 1851, Priest in 1856, and appointed Curate-in-Charge of Newtimber Sussex. Ouseley co-opted him as an Honorary Fellow of his collegiate choral foundation at St. Michael's Tenbury. He married in 1861 and became Vicar of Chippenham, a living under the patronage of his college. His induction took place on 25th March 1861. The Clergy List for 1863, valued the living at £284 p.a. (= £12,360), and names as his Curates: the Revds. James and Sidebottom, with whom he ministered to a parochial population of 4,819. He was to be appointed a Hon. Canon of Bristol from 1882, and served as Rural Dean of Chippenham from 1883-1899. He retired in 1904 to Lowden Lodge, continuing as Rector of Kellaways (a post he had held since 1884). In common with his predecessor, Lewis Purbick (who had died in office on 28 August 1860, aged 55), Rich and his family are buried at Tytherton Lucas, his wife having predeceased him in 1911. A man dedicated both to his ministry and marriage, he fathered a son and four daughters. Plates 26 & 27 show him first as a student, and then in old age, not unlike some benign headmaster replete with mortar board.

Plate 26: John Rich
(National Portrait Gallery)

Plate 27: Canon John Rich
(William Gaskell: Wiltshire Leaders)

Among his Oxford contemporaries just a year ahead of him, was The Revd. Sir Frederick Gore Ouseley (1825-1889, Plate 28) with whom he was to maintain a lifelong friendship through music, which was to have significant consequences for the Georgian organ in this church. Nicholas Temperley writes:[106]

'Ouseley's importance was not primarily as a composer. Simply by dedicating his rank and wealth to the musical profession, he helped to lay the foundations for the upward progress of English music which was already evident. His social position, though unaided by any marked force of personality, allowed him to secure for music recognition such as it had not enjoyed for generations. As professor at Oxford he made music a serious subject of study; as nominal founder and first president of the [Royal] Musical Association he established musicology (as it was later termed) as a respected field of learning. His own scholarship was distinguished, especially in Spanish theory and early English church music.'

Ouseley's most enduring monument is the College of St Michael and All Angels Tenbury Wells, which for over 100 years remained 'a model for the choral service of the church in these realms'. He lavished much of his wealth as well as his energy and devotion on the founding and nurturing of this institution. It was described in 1883 as 'the one real development of the aesthetic principle that England is yet able to boast' – a startling challenge to Victorian materialism and popular culture. He was also an expert on organ design and inspected 190 organs during a tour of Europe in 1848–9.

Yet in 1871 the diarist Revd. Francis Kilvert, attempted to belittle Ouseley's importance as a musician, musicologist and organ adviser as his 'hobby', furthermore he was unimpressed by a service he attended at St. Michael's College, Tenbury.

Plate 28: The Revd. Sir Frederick Gore Ouseley.

Plate 29 comprises what was probably the first interior photograph of the building and the only one to show the 1848 pews. Note the corporation pew, gas lit chandelier, the solid fuel stove heater to the right by the Prynne Memorial (stove pipe above). The Norman chancel arch is now above the clergy vestry. The presence of the choir stalls in the Chancel (a relatively recent loss) would suggest that this photograph was taken after the induction of John Rich.

Interior of Parish Church, looking East.
(From a Photograph before 1874.)

To face p. 24.

Plate 29: The interior looking East with the 1848 pews.

The young John Rich was intensely energetic, and as a musician he was a skilful 'cellist, had a fine bass voice, and gave great personal attention to the training of the choir. His obituary concluded that 'there is no doubt that due to his personal training the choir of the Parish Church always maintained a foremost position among church choirs of the country'.[107] His compositions are modest: a few chants have survived in manuscript (Plates 21 & 22).[108]

Kyries

Ex. 21: John Rich, Kyrie response 'St.Andrews.'

Ex. 22: John Rich, Double Chant in C.

He had started as he meant to go on: the *Wiltshire Independent* of April 23rd. 1863 reported that 'A meeting convened by a circular, was held in The New Hall ....for the purpose of taking into consideration, the small remuneration the respected organist Mr. Coombs (James Morris II), receives for his services, and does not amount to the sum of £15 (£674.40) yearly. The Revd. John Rich......expressed a wish that the sum of £50 a year (£2,158) could be subscribed amongst the pew holders of the church, and that £40 a year (£1,726.40) should be paid to the organist and the £10 surplus (£431.60) is given to Mr. Wilson's boys (Wilson was Headmaster of the National School who formed part of the choir and for supplying them with books etc.).

Thus under Rich's regime the changes in church music arising from the Oxford movement became fully established. Within this decade surpliced choirs leading services from chancel choir stalls grew apace, and Diocesan Choral Festivals were becoming institutionalised countrywide. By 1866 the choir in St Andrew's had donned surplices and were moved from the west gallery to chancel stalls. The pea-shooting pranks of the choir boys came to an end, as J. Lee Osborn later recalled in his profile of the town:

'The organ formerly stood in the gallery at the west end of the church; whence little boys of the choir (some still living) were wont to relieve the tedium of the service by playing pea-shooters artfully concealed between books on the young ladies of a local academy who occupied part of the gallery then in St. Catherine's Chapel [now the Baptistery].' [109]

After the failed attempt to move the Seede organ from the west gallery to the chancel in the 1852, a second organ, by Sweetland of Bath, was installed in the Lady Chapel (also known as the Baynton Chapel at that time). A self-contradictory account by the Churchwarden John Noyes of 1866 [110] had claimed that the Seede organ was 'unfit for further service.'[111] The specification of the Sweetland organ was as follows:[112]

One manual CC-f3, six stops throughout:

Open Diapason [8']

Stop Diapason (Treble and Bass) [8']

Viol da gamba [8']

Principal [4']

Twelfth [2 2/3']

Fifteenth [2']

Bourdon Pedals two octaves [CC-c1] 16'

The question of 'alterations in the west gallery for increasing the number of seatings therein' was again raised in the Vestry Minutes of 7th June and 9th August 1866, but no decision was taken.[113]

Although hymn singing had been officially approved in 1820, numerous local collections were compiled before the first edition of 'Hymns Ancient & Modern' was published in 1861. In 1868 the first Diocesan Festival [114] of choirs from the Chippenham district took place in St Andrew's. This received extensive coverage in the press which reflected the considerable change in aesthetics and attitudes towards music in the worship of parish churches since the eighteenth century:[115]

'An extraordinary revival in Church music and hymnody has taken place in this day. Our Church is bestirring herself with wonderful energy, and is producing, both from the devout melodies of her own children, and from the sacred stores of other churches, hymns of the most spiritual depth and expression, and music of great richness, sweetness and purity'.

The first festival of choirs in the Chippenham district took place on Thursday April 30th, 1868. The parishes in union with the Diocesan Choral Association are - Chippenham, Bowden Hill, Biddestone, Alderton, Grittleton, Broad Somerford, Seagry, Langley Fitzhurst, Kington St. Michael, Stanton St. Quintin, and Yatton Keynall. The number of voices is about one hundred and seventy: the choirs of Bowden Hill, Chippenham and Broad Somerford consist only of males. At 1.15 the choirs met for a rehearsal, and were skilfully arranged by the Rev. H.Palmer the local secretary: the male choirs in the chancel, the rest of the singers in the Baynton [Lady] Chapel, at the east of the south aisle; the trebles and alto in front; the tenors and basses behind. A short rehearsal then took place; and at half past three the choirs which were to occupy the Chancel consisting of about 40 boys and 25 men and 18 clergy in their surplices, &c., having formed a procession in the adjoining National School, entered the Church by the Western Door. Hymn 164 [*We love the place O God...*] Ancient and Modern[116], was sung by them in unison as they walked up the Nave of the Church accompanied on the great organ by Mr. Coombs, the worthy and respected organist of the parish. On reaching the chancel, the last two verses were sung in harmony, being taken up by the other choirs who had been previously placed in the side chapel. The hymn was sung with great precision and the effect felt to be solemn and inspiring. The Vicar [John Rich] then proceeded to sing the first part of the service [Evensong] (which was choral throughout), according to Tallis's arrangement. After the third collect followed Hymn 117 [Jesus lives!,.....] and the remainder of the prayers were intoned by the Rev. H.C.Palmer, Perpetual Curate of St. Anne's, Bowden Hill, and the Secretary to the Chippenham portion of the Association. Hymn 238 [*Now thank we all our God......*] was then sung, afterwhich followed an eloquent and very appropriate sermon by the Rev. Canon Barrow, Rector of West Kington who took the occasion to enforce upon the choirs the necessity of being reverent in the practising's, and that they should strive that all their singing should be to God's glory, and not for their own pleasure or man's praise. The service was closed by the singing of the 168th Hymn [To the name of our salvation], during which a collection was made in aid of the Association; and at the conclusion the Hallelujah chorus was played in a most spirited manner, by Mr. Coombs on the great organ.

The service was throughout accompanied by Mr. Rockton, the Association choirmaster, on a sweet but full-toned organ by Sweetland of Bath, which has been lately erected in the [Lady] Chapel.'

This report also contradicts Noyes's claim of 1866 that the Seede's 'grand organ' was 'unfit for further service' and confirms that Coombs was still in office, and the organ was still in playing order. This is not surprising since the instrument had received the attention from Holdich described above only fourteen years previously. He continued as organist until his retirement c.1867/8 and, as a freeholder, living in Ivy Lane, and attended the Vestry Meeting of July 1867. He died on 20th March 1873 at the age of 74. He is interred in the London Road Cemetery between two sons: an infant Charles who had died on 14th April 1869 aged 19 months; and Maurice E. Combs of Trinity Square London who died in 29th November 1875. James Maurice Coombs third son: Maurice E. Coombs had entered the medical profession, studied at University College, London, passing the examinations in anatomy and physiology of The Royal College of Surgeons of England.[117]

James Morris Coombs was succeeded by the youthful William Bradshaw (1852-1907) from Bath, and was to remain in the post for nearly forty years until his death. Although a musician himself, Rich had also taken professional advice from Ouseley over this appointment. Bradshaw was a budding professional, a pupil of James Kendrick Pyne (1810-1893), organist of Bath Abbey, and gained the L.R.A.M. and A.R.C.O. (July 1890) diplomas. He passed the playing section of the F.R.C.O. in January 1892 but did not continue to complete the written examination. His obituary (*North Wilts Guardian* 3 January 1908) also refers to his fine reputation as an organ recitalist and piano teacher, as well as to his careful tuition of the Chippenham Harmonic Society. A man of devotion to duty he was reported never to have missed a service during his thirty-six years in office, except during annual family holidays (*Wiltshire Telegraph* 4 Jan. 1908). He is commemorated by a brass plaque in the chancel adjacent to the site of the former Gray and Davison console. With the support of Rich the choir grew in strength.

Local newspapers of the 1870s carried details of church service lists. Below are those of the choral services held in St Andrew's on Palm Sunday, Good Friday and Christmas Day in 1875. [118] These relate to The Book of Common Prayer Services and give details of the composers and keys of the chants and occasional anthems. Almost of all the hymns are very familiar today. Note the predominance of minor key chants on Good Friday, also that the hymns have almost entirely disappeared from present day publications. Some items are in referred to as in MS which may indicate that they were composed by Coombs II or Rich:

PALM SUNDAY, - Morning Prayer and Holy Communion at 10.30 a.m. - Venite-Woodward in C; Beneficiate Omnia Opera , MS; Jubilate; Hymns 347 [Once only once...] 86 [All glory laud...] ; Kyrie, Coombs, in E; Creed, Best in A. Afternoon Prayer at 3p.m. - Hymn 196 [Guide me O thou great Redeemer...] Evening Service at 6.30 p.m.- Glorias and Deus Misereatur, Spofforth in G; Magnificat, Hopkins, in E; Hymns 87 [Ride on, ride on...], 172 [Hosanna to the Lord...], 276 [At even, ere the sun was set...] Offertories for Home Missions.

GOOD FRIDAY, - Morning Prayer at 10.30 a.m.- Venite, Purcell in A minor; Te Deum, No.10 in D minor; Benedictus, Flintoft in D minor; Hymn 91 [O'erwhelmed in depths of woe...] Kyrie in A minor; Hymn 100 [O come and mourn with me awhile]. Afternoon prayer at 3p.m. - Hymn 91. Evening Prayer, 7 p.m., - Gloria and Nunc Dimittis, Beethoven in C minor; Cantate, Cooke, in C minor; Hymns 104, [Saviour, when in dust to Thee] 100, 96 [In the Lord's atoning grief].

CHRISTMAS DAY, - Morning Prayer and Holy Communion at 10.30 a.m. - Hymn 43 [Hark the herald...], Venite Monk, in G; Te Deum, from Aldrich; Benedictus, MS in A; Anthem and Hymn 42 [O come all ye faithful]. Hymn, 46 [Of the Father's Love...],Creed, Stainer. Evening Service at 7p.m. - Hymn 44 [While shepherds watched] Psalms, Lord Mornington in Eb, and Battishill in Eb, Magnificat MS, in G; Deus Misereatur MS, in G; Anthem and Hymn 142 [Jerusalem the golden...] Hymns 43 [Hark the Herald...] 278 [Hail, gladdening light...]

The major achievement of Rich's incumbency was to be the extensive rebuilding and enlargement of the church completed in 1878. This was not planned in haste; he had given priority, and first addressed the condition of St Nicholas, Tytherton Lucas. The 1866 Vestry Meeting at Tytherton was reported in the *Wiltshire Independent*. [119]

'A Vestry Meeting was held on Thursday morning last, when the Churchwarden's Accounts were submitted and allowed. Mr. H[enry] B[roome] Pinneger was re-elected Churchwarden and he proposed a church rate which was heavily objected to by 5-1. In reply to a question from the Rev. J Rich as to the desirability of polling the Parish, his Churchwarden was of the opinion that it would be useless. The matter therefore fell to the ground.'

Undeterred, John Rich issued a circular letter in 1867:

'I am anxious to refloor and reseat the Church of Tytherton Lucas, a parish which, I believe the last 600 years annexed to Chippenham.

The church was almost entirely rebuilt at the beginning of this century [1802-3], and since that time the pews and flooring have probably remained untouched until a few years ago, when, through the liberality of a gentleman [Thomas Crook] in the neighbourhood, a small portion was well and substantially put in order: the rest is in a most dilapidated condition. The Chancel, I am about to restore myself; for the remainder of the work I must appeal chiefly to the kindness of friends.

The parish is small, and from the fact that the larger number of moneyed persons connected with it are not members of the Church of England, I can obtain but small help from it, viz. about £30. The sum required is from £150 to £200. [£6,855 - £9,140] If you can help me in raising this I shall feel grateful.

I am dear Sir, /yours faithfully, /John Rich.'

Returning to St Andrew's, it was in November 1874 at a public meeting, chaired by the Mayor, and held in the New Hall, that a major enlargement and reordering of St Andrew's was unanimously agreed to:

Ist. Enlarge the Parish Church by the addition of a North Aisle and Organ Chamber, and to restore the Chancel, and thereby to give an increased accommodation of about 320 unappropriated sittings.

2nd: To remove the unsightly Flat and Low Ceilings and upright columns, and to replace them with Open Timber Roofs and Arches to correspond with the general architecture of the church. Notice at this stage there is no mention of extending the Chancel or raising the height of the roof, moving the chancel arch, or of a North Door.

Plans have been prepared and estimates made, viz. for the whole work £6,000, [= £274,200 today] & for the first portion £4,000 [=£182,800]; it is hoped that eventually funds will be forthcoming to complete the whole.

The old Organ 'by Byfield and Harris' (this was the not unreasonable guess by Ouseley, to whom Rich had turned for advice) requires rebuilding, it being at present so much out of repair that it cannot be used; about £300 [£13,710; rather an underestimate as we shall see] is required for this.

A Working Committee was established comprising:

Mr. John Noyes, Mayor.

The Rev. J. Rich, Vicar.

West-Awdry Esq, Churchwarden.

Mr. W.A. Harries, Churchwarden.

Mr. I.C. Child, Sydesman.

A.J. Keary, Chairman of the Local Board.

A.B. Rooke Esq.

F. Goldney Esq. MP [120]

Ahead of this public meeting Rich had already approached the Incorporated Church Building Society over a grant. As a Government- sponsored institution (with offices in No.7 Whitehall) the I.C.B.S. was primarily concerned with providing free seating in places of worship to meet population growth. The protocol of applications is not dissimilar from many of the procedures we follow today in committees of the Church Buildings Council: - Faculty approval – details of proposed work – architects/builder's plans – parochial statistics – parochial resources – the population of the Parish is given as 5,202 of whom 3,000 were deemed to be Poor and received support from the Parish Poor Rate which in 1876 disbursed £1,203 9s 1p. This was today's equivalent of about £58,138.87.

His letter to the Incorporated Church Building Society of 29th October 1874 has some interesting additional details and observations:

'The present small chancel arch greatly impedes the sound, that is the object of removing it, but it is wished not to lose it, and it is proposed to place it at the entrance to the present vestry, which would then be available for invalids to hear the service and sit comfortably by a fire. [The fireplace can be still be seen in the vestry]. The screen is at present lying in the vestry in a dilapidated condition, the present East window is more cement than stone and we think it may be reworked but copied, or if it will bear it , restored and placed in the Organ Chamber as shown in the plans....The Western Arch to the Organ Chamber is made as high as possible as the plan will allow to let out the sound. [Unfortunately, this was to be of little advantage since the organ was turned at right angles to the arch and rebuilt to speak directly across the chancel as it continues to do today.] ...It is intended that the Chancel and Vestry be covered with stone tiling, the rest of the church slated, we cannot afford lead.'

He continued in an economical vein by recommending that a local Architect Robert Darley be employed as he could also act as Clerk of Works and so avoid travelling expenses. Rich secured £80 (£3,864.80) from the I.C.B.S. but this would only be released when the work was satisfactorily completed. Funds flowed in generously so that by July 1875 the work was begun by the builders, Smith and Light of Chippenham, to the design of local architects Richard Darley, brother of Robert. The I.C.B.S. plan number 1718; Plate 30 shows the new north aisle, the chancel lengthened by 20' and stepped up', and a new high altar and sanctuary with a further four steps up (the reredos was relegated to the choir vestry in the 1960s). The new east window was not installed until end of the century; not in 1878 as the current church guide states. Rich's account book for the fund-raising is in the Church deposit at the Wiltshire History Centre together with a list of subscribers to the church building and the restoration of the Seede organ.[121] The subscription list of 1878 at the reopening of the church contains 116 names who contributed a total of £5,845-4-0 to the cost of the building works, the most substantial sum, £2,000, coming from the Feofees of the Church Lands. However, a second parallel column reveals a stark indifference, in that only 42 of them contributed towards the rebuilding of the organ. Their total donations amounted to £113.06, far short of Gray & Davison's estimate of £800. The most generous donors to the organ were W.H. Poynder Esq. of Hartham Park (£50) and the Revd. Sir. Frederick Gore Ouseley, Bart. (£10 guineas).

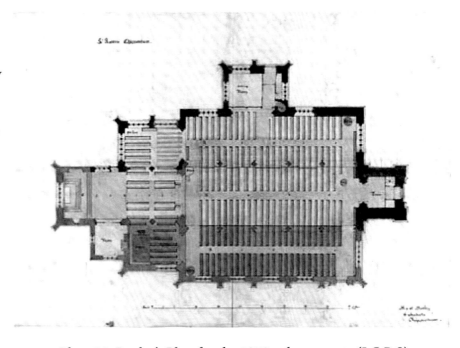

Plate 30: Darley's Plan for the 1878 enlargement. (I.C.B.S).

The diarist Francis Kilvert socialised with the Rich family. He wrote on 3rd January 1875 that at Holy Communion a poor man had taken the chalice and wished Rich ' A Happy New Year.' Later that year on 24th July, Kilvert noted that the foundations of the new north aisle were being dug: 'Draper Wharry's assistant told me that things were not managed nicely when the tombstones and graves were necessarily interfered with. He said scalps [with] hair still on them were left lying around and that he himself had seen a hedgehog tearing at the arm of a body which still had flesh upon it...'

A special service of Evensong was held on 23rd September 1876 (Trinity 15) at which 'Offertories were for 'Rebuilding Old Organ.' Work progressed towards a reopening of the church on Sunday 15th January 1878. The cost was £6,400 (=£309,184) with an estimated £600 (=£28,986) still required to rebuild the organ in the new North Aisle chamber.

Plate 31 shows the interior of the church in 1878. The 1921 war memorial screen, the present pulpit (1926) and the Lady Chapel screen (also built in 1921 from old roof timbers in memory of John Rich) are missing. Note the stone lectern (left) and the stone pulpit (right). Sweetland's organ is visible in the Lady Chapel, and the Council Pews which were retained until their removal in the early 1960s. How refreshing it is to see the graceful perpendicular architecture of the building unencumbered by 21st century speakers!

Plate 31: The interior looking East in 1878.

The Brice Seede organ awaits rebuilding and enlargement in its chamber, whereby hangs a painful tale. After his Trojan efforts to bring the church building project to fruition, an accident prevented John Rich from attending the opening services. *The Devizes & Wiltshire Gazette* [122] reported that on Thursday 10th January the organ had been moved from its former 'place of honour'[123] in the west gallery into the chamber to await rebuilding. Rich inspected the work the following morning. Noticing that one of the facade pipes was not correctly positioned, he climbed onto a seat to straighten it, but the seat had not been secured. He fell violently to the floor and fractured the cap of his shoulder joint 'causing him much pain and confinement to his room.' Rough justice perhaps for the unwise re-siting of the organ?

The church was duly reopened on 15th January 1878 and reported in extensive detail in the *Chippenham Chronicle*. [124] The service was accompanied by the small Sweetland organ, played by Theodore Bradshaw, reinforced by a quartet of brass instruments. Shortly afterwards Rich was visited by his friend Ouseley, who preached at Evensong on 17th January, and no doubt had further discussions took place with him on the rebuilding of the Seede organ.

The 1879 rebuild of the organ by Gray & Davison.

It was Ouseley's tour of European organs in 1851 that helped him to evolve a 'progressive conservative' approach in his advisory work. It is possible that the beautiful case and much of Seede's original pipework would not have survived without his cautious advice. An article in the Journal of The Royal College of Organists [125] shows that in that decade Ouseley took the same approach over the historic Smith pipework when advising E.J.Hopkins over instrument of the Temple Church. The influence of Ouseley is also evident from notes in the Estimate Ledgers of Gray & Davison of London, who were contracted to rebuild the organ, 'retaining the original case and as much of the original pipework as possible.' For example: there is a significant note that the Tierce rank was to be remain in the Sesquialtera stop. However, the St.Andrew's organ fund was still almost £500 (=£24,155) short of its target. Again, Rich's zealous energy came to the fore, and Civic support was also forthcoming: the Mayor proposed a fancy bazaar, and the final cost, which had risen from the original estimate of £600, to £941-01- 6d. [= £45,463.33] was eventually raised. John Rich had also taken an interest in the specification. He had twice visited the organ builder's workshop in Euston Road to 'order verbally' the deep 32' stop in the Pedal organ in February 1879, and again in July, for the gently voiced Viol da Gamba of the Choir Organ.

Plate 32: the organ as rebuilt 1879 by Gray & Davison (British Organ Archive).

*Plate 33: In case of wartime loss or damage the Seede case was officially photographed in 1941.
(National Monuments Record)*

It was largely thanks to the intervention of the late Michael Gillingham, founding Chairman of The British Institute of Organ Studies[126] in 1976 that the business records of Gray & Davison escaped destruction when the firm ceased trading in 1971. These, together with those of some other leading nineteenth century organ builders, were to form the foundation of the British Organ Archive.[127] This invaluable resource is now located in the Cadbury Research Centre at the University of Birmingham under the joint aegis of B.I.O.S. and the R.C.O.

The Gray & Davison factory book contains the following entry on St Andrews:

Organ No.10412 Chippenham Parish Church. Rebuilding and enlarging the organ retaining the existing case and pipes as far as available. 3 manuals overhanging - CC-a [3] and Pedal - radiating and concave CCC - f[1] . If the doorway on the east side of organ is inconvenient it may be blocked-up.

Great Organ

Double Diapason 16ft. - New throughout.

Open Diapason 8ft. - Old part (part new).

53

Spitz Flute 8ft. - Tapering (new).

Clarabella, Stopped Bass 8ft. - Wood through, Old.

Harmonic Flute 4ft. - Metal through (new).

Twelfth 2 2/3ft. old.

Fifteenth 2 ft. old.

Sesquialtera 3 ranks Various old. To remain as they are with the tierce.

Furniture 2 ranks Various old.

Trumpet 8ft. Metal through [part new?]

Clarion 4ft. Metal through [new]

Swell Organ

Lieblich Bourdon 16ft Wood through. Not more than 7 [pipes] outside [the swell-box]

Open Diapason 8ft. Not more than 7 [pipes] outside [the swell-box]

Stopped Diapason 8ft. Metal [old] treble and Wood bass [new] 19 notes [pipes] painted.

Keraulophon (grooved) 8ft. Metal tenor C.

Voix Celeste 8ft. Metal tenor C. No cancelled 24/2/1879

Principal 4ft. Metal through.

Fifteenth 2ft. Metal through

Mixture 4 ranks Metal through

12-15-19-22 CC - f [2]

1-8-12-15 f#[2] - a [3] 10 top notes [?]

Cornopean 8ft. Metal through.

Clarion 4ft. Metal through.

Tremulant No. 24/2/1879.

Choir Organ

Dulciana 8ft. Metal through.

Viol da gamba 8ft. ordered verbally by Mr. Rich July 1879.

Stopped Diapason 8ft. Wood through - old - 8 lower notes [pipes] painted CC to G.

Gemshorn 4 ft. Metal through.

Flute 4 ft. Wood - old.

Piccolo 2 ft. Wood through.

Clarinet 8ft. Metal through.

Pedal Organ

1. Sub-Bourdon 32ft. ordered 25.2.1879.

2. Open Diapason 16ft. Wood through.

3. Stopped Diapason 16ft. Wood through.

4. Violoncello 8ft. Metal through.

5. Trombone 16ft. Broad [wood] tubes

Couplers

Swell to Great

Swell to Choir

Choir to Great

Swell to Pedal

Great to Pedal

Choir to Pedal

Five composition pedals, 3 to Great and 2 to Swell.

A new front toward chancel to be provided in oak. Pipes in both fronts to be decorated or gilded.

20th February , 1879.

The Gray & Davison ledger of 23rd September concludes the account as follows:

'To rebuilding organ no. 10412 of 3 manuals and pedals adapting the existing case to North Aisle and retaining pipes as far as available there, and throughout the organ. A new front of oak in chancel of decorated pipes. Erected complete as per estimate.

Estimate no. 475: £800-00-0

A Contra Bourdon CCCC 32ft. fixing etc. £80-00-0

lower octaves zinc Double Diapason to Great previously

estimated for. £35-00-0

Rearranging Swell Mixture. £5-00-0

A Gamba to Choir, fixing. £25-00-0

2 extra dumb pipes to aisle front, carriage and packing etc. £7-10-0

A pine stool, stained and varnished. £1-11-6

Paid cash December 21st. £ 604-00-0

Balance December 31st. £ 350-01-6

Total: £ 954- 01-6

October 22nd, 1879.

10 extra dumb pipes in front of zinc. £6

Decoration and fitting. £8

Further documentation was discovered by a team of N.A.D.F.A.S Church Recorders, in use as a clergy vestry drawer lining during 2013. This comprised a drawing of the widening of the Seede case and a more elaborate design for the lintel above the present entrance to the choir vestry. This is reproduced as Plate 34.

Plate 34: Gray & Davison's plan for the widening of the case.

There was a choice between gilding or diapering the new front pipes (zinc). The latter was chosen, but stripped off in 1965. Gilding would have been more apt for the Seede case but would have been more expensive compared with Gray & Davison's standard stencilling. The wind supply was generated by a pair of hydraulic engines worked from the borough water supply.

The opening service of the rebuilt organ was held on 23rd September 1879. The inaugural recital was given by George Riseley (1845-1899), organist of Bristol Cathedral, also a concert organist with a contiguous civic appointment at the Colston Hall. He gave a series of recitals in the Royal Albert Hall in 1885, and later became a professor of organ at the Royal Academy of Music. His recital in Chippenham on 23rd September was reported in The *Chippenham Chronicle* of 26th September. The latter described the organ thus: 'Its tone is most pleasing – rich, full and lively; powerful, yet not overpowering.' It is not improbable that the final phrase is a suggestion that the edge of the tone was muffled by the cramped layout of the instrument in the new chamber location. Riseley's programme was follows: Sonata No.5 in D Mendelssohn; Andante by Edouard Silas; J.S. Bach's 'Grand Fugue G minor' (BWV 542); Guilmant's March on '*Lift up your heads*' from *Messiah* and 'An Air with Variations by Haydn' (possibly an arrangement of the third movement of the 'Emperor Quartet', Op.76 No.3).

In the following year the small Sweetland organ was advertised for sale in the *Western Daily Press*.[128]

'FOR SALE, the small ORGAN now in Chippenham Parish Church: one manual CC-F, six stops throughout - Open Diapason, Stop Diapason (Treble and Bass) Viol da gamba, Principal, Twelfth, Fifteenth. Bourdon Pedals two octaves, builder Sweetland Bath. This organ is suitably voiced for a large building and is in thorough repair to be sold as the old organ having been rebuilt. Lowest price £80 [= about £3,864.80].

Apply to Mr. Bradshaw, Chippenham, Wilts.'

It would be wrong to assume that the removal of organs from acoustically ideal west gallery, (or free standing floor locations), to musically insensitive chancel chambers during the Victorian period was not met without vigorous critical debate at the time in relation to both Cathedrals and Parish Churches.

In 1855, S.S. Wesley wrote to the editor of *The Salisbury and Winchester Journal as follows*:

Sir, - One of your contemporaries, some time since, contained an announcement of its being the intention of the Dean and Chapter of Salisbury to move the organ from the choir screen to the side of the choir of their cathedral. The profession to which I belong being rarely consulted on such a subject, and knowing well as I do, that such a step is highly detrimental to musical effect, I take this means of expressing my opinion, that not only is the effect of an organ injured by being placed at the side, instead of the centre of a cathedral, but the choir service also suffers in various ways. [129]

By the next decade the debate featured in architectural periodicals. In 1867 the architect and musician F. H. S[utton]. (1820-1873) wrote in *Church Builder:*[130] 'As regards the ......sound of the instrument itself, no doubt a place at the west end of a church, or over a choir screen, is by far the best, for then its tones are able to expand in all directions....it is almost impossible not to look back with a sort of half regret upon the stately cases with their rich towers and pilasters...'

It had remained a contentious issue in through the 1870s when *The Musical Times*[131] compared Cavaillé-Coll's organ for Sheffield's Albert Hall unfavourably with British church organs:

' ...Which architects, with the consent of the clergy , contrive to thrust into holes at the east end of the edifice ; and where the organ builder, with his high pressures, makes the pipes scream revengefully on the assembled congregants.'

The architect and musician H.H. Statham (1839-1924) wrote in *The Church Builder* in 1873:[132]

'We never see one of the 'organ chambers' which is the fashion to build [in].....our modern churches, as a serious blunder. It suited the clergy and choir in the chancel......[but] the quality of tone must be injured when the pipes have not space to speak out freely, and that is a serious matter.'

These words are equally true today in relation to the future of the organ of the parish church of St. Andrew's, Chippenham. It was fortunate that the vicar John Rich was a musician and a close friend of Frederick Gore-Ouseley (who preached at Evensong on 17th January 1878) whose historical awareness related the instrument to the school of Harris & Byfield in whose steps Brice Seede followed. Moving organs from music - friendly west galleries to tonally suffocating organ chambers from the mid-C19th was as contentious as the reverse process can be today.

Ouseley launched a furious attacked on north aisle chambers in a paper to the Royal Musical

Association in 1886, also the year of his election as President of The Royal College of Organists. Today we have reason to be very grateful that he advised Rich to retain as much of Seede's pipework as possible. It was very much the precedent set by Ouseley that determined the approach advocated in the failed 'St. Andrew's Project' of 2003-2005. The note in Gray & Davison's factory book that the mixture compositions were 'to remain as they are with the tierce' certainly stems from Ouseley. In 1886, his final protest was delivered, not as a priest, but as a musician, organ adviser and historian, in which he roundly condemned organ chambers, both as Professor of Music at Oxford and the founding President of the Royal Musical Association, in a paper read in London on 1st February 1886:

'Ordinary parish churches and chapels, in many cases, are so constructed that the only available place for the organ consistent with pure tone, the 16' pipes are usually so hidden away behind the instrument that they are scarcely audible in the church, while the mixtures seem doubly shrill and strident by contrast. Moreover, the mechanism is often inconveniently overcrowded, causing frequent derangement and cypherings, and the bellows are often injured by damp in so confined a space … I must once and for all, utter my indignant protest against organ chambers……. 'There are first the interests of the clergy, who regard the matter, perhaps, from an ecclesiological point of view. Then there are the interests of the singers…Next we have the interest of the organist from a comparatively instrumental aspect. After him comes the architect, who chiefly looks at the appearance of the case, and too frequently hates the organ entirely, and would fain conceal it as much as possible. Lastly there is the organ builder who feels that his reputation is more or less dependent on the decision as to the locality to which those who have the management of the affair shall finally come. Here is, then, a fruitful source of quarrels and differences, of contentions and recriminations, of jealousies and reviling, or grumbling and discontent. [133]

However given, Ouseley's position as a priest, organist and composer, he was between a rock and a hard place. As a clergyman it would be unprofessional of him to have interfered too overtly with Canon Rich's ecclesiological plans for St Andrew's.

Gray & Davison's order book of 20th September 1894 records additional work to the instrument: 'To cleaning & repairing organ; putting a Gamba 8ft in place of Spitz Flute; putting concussion bellows to Choir organ; £56.10.0.'

The other important legacies of Canon Rich's incumbency were enlargement of the Church School, building of the Mission Chapel of St Peter's, Lowden and its associated school, not to mention his sensitive and generous ministry to the poor. Further details of Rich's life can be found in the extensive press obituaries and in the chapter devoted to him in William Gaskell's book *Wiltshire Leaders*.[134] The choir had become sufficiently numerous to be divided into two sections: one part undertakes to lead the congregation in the musical portions of the services of the Parish Church, the other at St Peter's Mission Church in Lowden. A record of the choir's repertoire survives in the organist's bound volume of 569 pages containing 80 anthems arranged in liturgical order. [135] This gives an overview of the repertoire accumulated during the times of Rich and Bradshaw. In editions published entirely by Novello & Co., not without some indifferent Victorian settings issued as *Musical Times* supplements, it contains editions of works by Farrant, Purcell, Croft, Handel, Haydn, Ouseley, Macfarren, Mendelssohn, Stainer and S.S. Wesley and Michael Wise.

The Early Twentieth Century

This began badly. Gray & Davison were required urgently in March 1900 as rainwater had leaked through the roof onto the Great soundboard.[136] This was removed and overhauled and they also carried out further cleaning and repair work. This included 'bushing couplers, compositions and pedal action [at a cost of] £39.10.0.' The company continued to tune the organ at £8 guineas per annum until 1905.

A further aspect of William Bradshaw's career was as an organ teacher. The Churchwarden's Account transcriptions of Harry Ross[137] contain a note of an income of £5 for water used by Mr. Bradshaw's pupils. The hydraulic blowing plant was proving expensive to maintain: in 1905 £97-16-3 was spent on this, and £9-10-4 on the water supply. Bradshaw's Annual Stipend was then £60.

This was to be the first of several occasions when it was clear that Darley's roof design above the organ chamber was unsatisfactory. This recurred on at least four occasions over the next 110 years, when snow was not swept from the chamber roof before it thawed. On each occasion the Great organ soundboard required dismantling and yet another overhaul in an organ builder's workshop. Yet the roof repairs were not always effective: snow melt flooded the organ in 1954 (see below). Two instances are documented as follows: first, a letter from the Architect Oswald Brakespear to the builders Hulbert Light & Co. Ltd. of 15th August 1964: [138]

> Dear Sirs,
> The P.C.C. is anxious to ensure that the organ chamber roof is completely sound and watertight. To do this it will I think be necessary :
>
> a. To strip the slates and relay with treated battens and counter battens on untearable felt, making up deficiencies with new slate and supplying new crease as required.
>
> b. To overhaul all leadwork, making up deficiencies, repairing by lead burning as necessary,
>
> c. To supply duckboards in both gutters made of treated softwood, except the longitudinal runners which should be of hardwood - not oak.
>
> Would you kindly let us have an estimate for this, inserting provisional sums for new slates and lead repairs if necessary.

Second, after storm damage in September 1990, Brakespear was again in contact with the building contractors Downing, Rudman & Bent, whose estimate for repairs was £7,920. However, in February 1991 they submitted the following note to the church:

'The damage found to have been done to the Organ Chamber Roof proved considerably more extensive than had been apparent when the estimate was prepared. £1,129.00 had been allowed but some renewals of fractured timber and, more particularly steelwork to repair main timbers that had been split were involved.'

Finally, in 2012 the organ chamber roof was redesigned and rebuilt under the direction of the architect Christopher Romain.

The Choir Vestry was added in 1907. Darley's plan shows its former position to have been in the south aisle chapel which is now the Baptistery. The same year saw the retirement of W.T.Bradshaw and his death at the age of 55 on 28th December. He received extensive obituaries in the local press:

The North Wilts Guardian [139]

'... In addition to being organist of the Parish Church, he was conductor of The Chippenham Harmonic Society and under his careful direction it attained a high position.....throughout his 39 years residence in Chippenham was always held in the highest esteem and respect, not only by the parishioners, but also by the residents of the town....He was a Freemason....[and] always took the keenest interest in anything for the welfare of the town in which he resided.'

The Wiltshire Telegraph [140]

'It is with deep regret that we have to record the death of Mr. William Theodore Bradshaw at his residence, Station Hill, at half past two o'clock on Saturday morning. The deceased who was 55 years of age, had a paralytic seizure on the previous Saturday morning, from which he did not recover. Mr. Bradshaw, who has gifts of the highest order, was a native of Bath, and came to Chippenham at the early age of 16 years, to occupy the responsible position of the Parish Church. During the whole of the 36 years he held that office, with the exception of his annual holiday, he never once missed a service, and his devotion to duty was one of the most prominent traits of his character. He was an Associate of the Royal College of Organists [and a Licentiate of the Royal Academy of Music], and his skill as an organist was recognised by the large attendance at the recitals which he gave at intervals. As a teacher of the pianoforte he was most successful, many of his pupils gaining high honours. There is much sympathy with the widow and family, who mourn the loss of a loving husband and kind father..'.

Today, in the Choir Vestry can normally be seen some brass plaques recording the 'Honour List of Attendances' of individual members of the choir during the early 20th century.

Bradshaw's successor in 1907 was a Mr. F.H. Hinton at a salary of £40 per annum. In the Church's Annual Report for 1908-9 [141] the Vicar wrote:

'Since this time last year [Spring 1908] the choir has increased considerably in numbers and there has been a corresponding improvement in the quality of singing. This I have no hesitation in ascribing on the one hand to Mr, Hinton, and to the readiness of both the men and boys on the other to devote time and trouble to the practices. I look forward to more younger men understanding their work for God in a more devotional spirit. When they realise the responsibility of their office.'

His resignation and the appointment of his successor were recorded in the Vicar's report of Easter 1914:

'In the course of the year Mr. Hinton resigned his office of organist and choirmaster of the Parish Church. Throughout the five years in which he held the post he spared no time, trouble or pains to render worthily the services of God's House. More than this, he ever set an example of reverence. At the time the Vicar and Churchwardens conveyed to Mr. Hinton their feeling of gratitude not only for the good work he had done in circumstances of considerable difficulty, but also for the way he had done it. I feel that these expressions will to-day be endorsed by the Vestry. Mr. Douglas Taylor, A.R.C.O., who was for some time assistant-organist of Winchester Cathedral, [and subsequently organist of St. Jude's Wolverhampton] was appointed in his place. Mr. Taylor is doing good work, the choir is working well under him: and he, as we all are, must be very pleased with the results of his efforts.'

At the Vestry Meeting of 8 April 1915 'Mr. Brotherhood reported that the initial expense of putting in electric apparatus to blow the organ would be something like £75.[142]

Taylor who drew a salary of £53-15.0 in 1916-1917 with a payment of £16.5.0 to his deputy Mr. Dear. In 1915, Taylor also engaged in correspondence with Harrison & Harrison of Durham relating to urgent repairs and tonal alterations to the instrument. Although these were not implemented because of wartime financial pressures it gives many insights not only into Taylor's tonal wishes, which were characteristic of the ethos of the late Romantic British organ, but also of the 'progressive conservative' outlook of Harrisons during that period. Of greater significance are Arthur Harrison's criticisms of Gray & Davison's interior layout of the instrument and his recommendations for a rearrangement. These remain pertinent today if the organ is to remain in its stifling chamber and become more overt in its tonal projection into the Nave, rather than returned to an optimal musical and tonal location in a west gallery. Tonally, Arthur Harrison recognised and valued the presence of the 18th and much of the 19th century pipework. However, by the turn of the century the preferred style for reed timbres had changed in favour of strong and smooth 'harmonic trebles.'

Arthur Harrison examined the instrument on 21st October 1915 and his company wrote to Taylor as follows:

REPORT ON THE ORGAN IN THE PARISH CHURCH, CHIPPENHAM.

E. Douglas Taylor Esq.,
24, Marshfield Road,
Chippenham.

Dear Sir,

Mr. Arthur Harrison examined the organ in the Parish Church on Thursday last the 21st inst. and as required by Mr. Hulbert, we now beg to submit a report and scheme for the consideration of the Church Council.

Although the organ is old-fashioned in construction and its mechanism is clumsy and worn out, yet it contains many valuable parts, a number of its pipes being good and some even of historic interest. Mr. Harrison found in it several stops that are obviously of late 17th or early 18th century workmanship. They doubtless belonged to the organ that formerly stood at the West end of the church, of which the old case, now facing West formed the front, and which we understand is said to have been the work of the famous English organ builder Renatus Harris. These stops should be carefully restored and preserved. There is also much other good material in the organ.

The antiquated and clumsy mechanism, however, is not the only defect. The sounding-boards are in a bad state and are full of "runnings"; the wind arrangements are poor and in a deplorable condition, and this applied not only to the hydraulic engines but also to the bellows, trunks, wind chests and indeed all the winding arrangements throughout the organ. The reed stops are also very unsatisfactory, the tone being uneven and harsh and coarse in quality. They compare very unfavourably with the rest of the pipework. Further, the organ is not well laid out, and it is impossible properly to get at some parts of it for tuning purposes.

We do not think that it would be a satisfactory plan merely to renew the mechanism and substitute electric motors for the hydraulic engines, at a cost of say £800 or £700. There are strong reasons why this course must not be taken. Obviously the defects of the organ would stand out all the more. And to apply new mechanism to the existing sound-boards and other defective structural parts would be sheer waste of money, for when the organ came to be properly rebuilt, as would have to be done before long, the mechanism would [have] to be remake [sic] at considerable extra expense to fit the new conditions.

The organ is worthy of the best treatment and we advise that it be dealt with as a whole. It ought to be thoroughly rebuilt from to[p] to bottom, the sounding-boards remade and renewed where necessary, with entirely new mechanism and winding arrangements on scientific principles, new reed stops inserted in place of the present ones, and all the good pipe-work carefully restored and regulated and fitted with tuning slides to prevent damage from tuning in the future. Certain stops ought to be revoice[d] and re-scaled where necessary in order to make the tonal scheme perfect and ensure the best musical effect be obtained from it.

This is a much more comprehensive and therefore more costly scheme than we understand has been contemplated, but we are of the opinion that it is the only plan that could prove really satisfactory. If it is at all possible for such a scheme to be entertained at the present time it is very advisable that it should not be postponed, for the organ is undoubtedly in a bad way and will rapidly get worse.

This scheme if artistically carried out, would leave the organ a thoroughly well equipped and up to date instrument, containing certain parts of special historic interest, and one worthy in every way of the fine church in which it stands. It would be a very much more durable organ than it has been in the past.

With regard to position and space, we think it would be a distinct advantage if the organ were built under the arches opening into the chancel and the player sitting under the westernmost arch where it would be seen to better advantage and every part of it made more accessible. A good wide passage could be left behind the organ for the choir to pass along.

We enclose, as requested, a full detailed specification and estimate [q.v.Appendix II] for carrying out the work on the above lines , together with particulars and estimate from Messrs. Watkins and Watson of London for an Electric Discus Blowing plant suitable and adequate for the restored organ.

Mr. Harrison would be glad at any time to call and discuss the matter further with the Church Authorities.

We are, dear Sir,
Yours faithfully,
Harrison & Harrison.

DURHAM 28th October 1915.[143]

Taylor evidently queried some of Arthur Harrison's tonal proposals. Although his letter to Harrisons has not survived, their reply has (q.v. Appendix III), and it gives interesting insights of the firm's tonal style and aesthetics of the period. [144]

Taylor held the post until 1923 when he moved to St. James's Tunbridge Wells where he remained until ca.1950. The exigencies of the Great War had led to the neglect of organ maintenance, an expenditure of £60 is recorded in the accounts of 1917-1918.[145] By 1920 the organist's salary had increased to £87.

R.H. Mather, F.R.C.O. was appointed organist and choirmaster in the autumn of 1923, but resigned on 7th June 1925 to take up an appointment at Walton Parish Church, Liverpool. The Vicar reported that 'He has been appreciated as a brilliant recitalist' was this perhaps coded clerical language implying that he had been less successful with the choir? Or, his response to an unsuccessful bid for an increase in his salary which he made to the P.C.C. in 1924? He was active as an accompanist and soloist with local music societies: for the Calne Music Society he performed J.S.Bach's Fantasia and Fugue in G minor (B.W.V. 542), 'Evensong' by Bairstow and a Fantasia in E by Silas.[146]

Mather's successor was announced in the *Parish Magazine* of July 1925 in which the Vicar wrote:

'After careful consideration and consultation with the Churchwardens , Members of the Choir and others, I have offered the vacant post to Mr. F.Ellerton (Mus. Bac.) New College, Oxford, F.R.C.O. and will probably be able to come here by about July 20th. Mr. Ellerton has been for the last four years organist and choirmaster at Hemel Hempstead Parish Church, Herts, and previous to that at St. Matthew's Redhill. I have had a great number of applications and I am sure you will all be thankful that I have been able to secure a man of great experience and responsibility. May I ask that you all do your best to procure pupils for him as I have assured him that there will be plenty of scope in the town and neighbourhood for a teacher of his ability.'

An undated photograph of c.1935 ? (Plate 35) may possibly have been taken on the occasion of Ellerton's departure.

Plate 35: The choir, organist, churchwardens, sacristan, verger and clergy ca.1935.

It is not untypical of organ histories that extensive periods of tenure by an organist are followed by alterations to instruments, sometimes essential, but not infrequently unnecessary. There is no documentation that the organ of St Andrew's received a major overhaul during the tenure of Bradshaw, nor did the problems of the Great War allow for regular maintenance. Although Harrison & Harrison had been invited to carry out an inspection and submit an estimate for restoration during 1915 the War prevented any action.

In February 1920 the instrument was inspected by Dr. Walter Alcock, organist of Salisbury Cathedral, whose findings for the Organ Committee were published in the *Parish Magazine*[147]

[Alcock] gave a report in which he said that the mechanism was very bad, the wind supply inadequate, the blowing apparatus very bad, and that while some of the pipes were worth preserving, the reeds were, without exception, the worst he had ever heard, and the sound boards were very bad with the wind leaking in all directions.

There is no reason to doubt any of Alcock's report, which accords with the main details of Arthur Harrison's of 1915, except that his condemnation of the reeds could reflect the fact that he presided over the fine Henry Willis organ in Salisbury whose suave style of reed voicing was very different from the brightness of Gray & Davison's as can be heard today in the historically informed restorations of their instruments at St. Anne's, Limehouse and Usk Parish Church. The same magazine report continues as follows:

'In 1920 the church was seriously in debt in many directions ... since then the state of the Organ has gradually become worse , and is now in a condition, as is well known, it has frequently broken down during services and it may at any time permanently do so...from which it appears that the cost will not be less than £1,100.... If these urgent repairs are to be carried out (and no one who attends the Parish Church can question the urgency) it is necessary that the Parochial Church Council, before commencing the work, should receive such support by way of subscriptions or promises...'

A Parochial Church Council meeting discussed the question of 'renovation' on 22nd August 1921.[148] During this problematic period the Chippenham music retailer and organ builder, Arthur Spencer was frequently called on to administer first aid as problems occurred. Spencer had been a colleague, or trainee of John Housley Adkins of Derby (1869-1947) before moving to Chippenham c.1904, when he acquired the business of G.E. Taylor trading as 'The Music Warehouse' from 13 Market Place until 1952.

The quality and ethos of his work as an organ builder were undistinguished, compromising the integrity of perfectly adequate village church instruments with unnecessary additions, alterations and enlargements.[149]

The matter appears to have been shelved for five years until the meeting of 12th December 1926, when concern was again expressed 'at the very serious condition' of the organ, shortly after the appointment of W. Ellerton as organist from 1925-1935. The need for an electric blower to replace the hydraulic engine was arguable, but the agenda to change the keyboard and stop-actions of the instrument from mechanical to pneumatic was a characteristic wish of organists of the period who found the weight of poorly regulated Victorian tracker actions physically challenging.

After a further inspection on 12th January 1927 two estimates were received on 10th May from Harrison & Harrison: one of £3,964 for 35 speaking stops 'and the old organ' and the other of £3,096 'and the other for 27 speaking stops 'and old organ.' These estimates did not include the installation of an electric blower. It was fortunate that these estimates exceeded the wherewithal of the church as notwithstanding the fine craftsmanship and musical integrity of the company this was not a period noted for historically informed regard for heritage organs. This was the age of 'The Imperial Organ'[150] founded on the tonal style of Henry Willis (d.1901) developed further through the influences of Hope-Jones and Col. Dixon. The details of Harrisons' proposals are given as Appendices II and III. [151]

Ellerton next obtained an estimate of £1,750 from G.H.C. Foskett of London to reconstruct the organ with an electric blowing plant in an outside pit. This was discussed on 15th July 1927 and was considered more feasible, but funds were still wanting, and the possibility of a Carnegie Trust Grant, or of a loan from the Feofees, were considered. The reality of the situation was that the Parish Organ Fund stood at just £28.3.9.

On 29th September 1927 Ellerton tabled estimates from J.C. Haskins of Bristol of £827 for renovating the organ and of £83-10-0 for a [Swell Organ] Voix Celeste and a further [Great Organ] Open Diapason, plus the cost of a Discus electric blower at £118, which totalled £1,029. An appeal for funds was launched in 1928, the 'thermometer' for which reached just £280 by early October. A gift day was held in November and an entertainment was presented in the Neeld Hall. On 7th October 1929 Arthur Spencer submitted a formal estimate for converting the instrument completely to pneumatic action and for installing an electric blower. It was agreed to delay any decision on this until an estimate had been obtained from Griffen and Stroud of Bath which amounted to £703.

Ellerton next visited the workshop of Adkins in Derby and reported to the P.C.C. Organ Committee that he had tested several of the organs constructed and renovated by them. They submitted an estimate for the same work of £570, excluding certain extras costed at £45. This was accepted unanimously by the Committee on 3rd March 1930. This is hardly surprising as the printed 'Statement of Accounts' for 1929 records that the organ fund amounted to £528-14-10. Arthur Spencer was then formally thanked 'for his readiness to appear in cases of emergency to enable the organ to function.'

Adkins began work in March 1931 installing an electric blower and pneumatic actions. To allow a Gamba to be added to the Swell Organ, the Gray & Davison Keraulophon was moved to the Great Organ in place of their Spitz Flute. A year later Ellerton was accorded a bonus of £7 guineas in recognition of his services with the organ restoration.[152]

These ten years of patient fund raising spanned the serious post-war depression that had crippled the economy by 1921-22. In the ensuing stagnation, skilled craftsmen, including organ builders were not excluded. Finally with the General Strike of 1926 and' The Great Depression' of 1929 the economy went from bad to worse.

Ellerton was succeeded as organist at St Andrew's for just two years (1935-1937) by W.H. Fithyan. He was followed by John Cecil Tomlins, who, after being Fithyan's assistant, held the post for 45 years until his retirement in 1982, and was the longest- serving organist of the 20th century. John Tomlins was born in Shrewsbury on 6th May 1910 and began organ studies at the age of twelve under Austin Herbert of St. Chad's Church, who also taught at the Birmingham School of Music. On leaving school, John was apprenticed to Forrests of Shrewsbury as a piano and organ tuner; he moved to Chippenham in 1930 to take up a tuning appointment with Campbell & Wells. Before his appointment to St. Andrew's he was organist at Sutton Benger Church. A year after gaining the teaching diploma of Trinity College, London he was appointed assistant organist

St Andrew's and became organist and choirmaster on the departure of Fithyan. During his war service as an R.A.F. telephonist he was stationed in Iceland, Belgium and The Netherlands. As the allies were converging on Berlin he received an order to report to the liberated Belsen concentration camp to tune a piano for the recreation of the medical services who were engaged in harrowing relief work.

It is also of considerable significance that during the 1939-1945 conflict the Seede case was photographed for the National Monuments Record as a precaution against its destruction by bombing. Whilst John Tomlins was serving away Mr.Dear, organist of St Peter's, Lowden, and Mr. Hussey deputized. The P.C.C. extended their to thanks to them when John Tomlins returned to his appointment in February 1946.[153] He subsequently continued organ studies with Clifford Harker of Bristol Cathedral and gained an A.R.C.M. in organ performance in 1951.

The later Twentieth Century.

Following his induction on 23rd November 1946 the Revd. Philip Snow (Vicar 1946-1978), himself a former boy chorister of Christ Church, took a close interest in the choir which had continued during the 1939-1945 conflict. In 1948 the reservoir of the organ required remedial attention and an estimate of £75 by Hele & Co. of Plymouth, who held the tuning contract, was declined in favour of one from Rushworth and Dreaper. Their estimate for only four days work, including tuning, was accepted. John Tomlins, having expressed dissatisfaction with the standard of Hele's tuning, their contract was terminated, and on 15th September 1948 they were asked cease their visits. No formal contract has been located. The responsibility passed to Rushworth & Dreaper at £14 gns. p.a. from 21st January 1949, raised to £18 gns. in 1951. John Tomlins's hard work with the choir was rewarded with an increase in his annual stipend from £58 to £78. [£1,800].

Performances of *Messiah* were given in the church in 1951 and 1952 under the aegis of the Chippenham and District Society of Arts Committee, (with funding from the Arts Council of Great Britain) chaired by a future St Andrew's Churchwarden, Cyril Rowley. The performance was conducted by Michael Vickers the Director of the *Wiltshire Rural Music School*. The programme contains lists of all performers of which there were members of ten choirs totalling 125 singers. The 1951 proceeds were towards the formation of a ''Chippenham Philharmonic Society' but in 1952 this had become the newly formed 'Chippenham Choral Society.' After a decade this was disbanded. During the mid-1980s the 'Chippenham Cantata [Choir] was formed, but without competent professional direction this also failed after almost twenty-five years. Yet choral societies continue to flourish in each of the neighbouring North Wiltshire towns and in several of the larger villages.

Plate 36: Programme of the 1951 Festival of Britain performance of Messiah.

The post-war recovery continued and choir and organ of St. Andrews had reached a satisfactory standard for the BBC West Home Service to relay an outside broadcast of Evensong on Passion Sunday, 30th March 1952.[154]

Philip Snow included in the printed order of service some telling instructions for choir and congregation:

1. Join firmly and steadily in the said parts of the Service, Confession, Creed, etc,

2. Sing the responses light and fairly fast.

3. Do not "drag" the hymns...

Finally: "...maintain COMPLETE SILENCE until the Organist ceases to play."

However, it was evident that the organ was again in need of further attention and in the Finance Committee minutes of 5th May 1953 the Vicar urged action as follows: 'Steps should be taken now to start such a fund to prepare for the time when a large sum will be required for essential work on the organ.' John Tomlins was asked to set up an old organ pipe as a collecting receptacle for a collection fund.[155]

Following further snow melt damage during the winter of 1954 Rushworth & Dreaper were required to overhaul the Great Organ soundboard at a cost of £155.156 An extra roof over the organ was proposed at a cost of £18.10, but the Finance Committee were not convinced that it would be a satisfactory solution. Meanwhile, by July 1957 the organ fund amounted to £124.8s.11d.

The 1965 rebuild by Percy Daniel & Co.

This decade was not blessed with our present cultural values of conservation, and where necessary, historically sensitive restorations of many aspects of our heritage. In Chippenham, this period saw the ruthless destruction of the elegant Georgian bridge over the River Avon and the demolition of several historic buildings. The organ of St. Andrew's Church was also to suffer in a time warp reflecting the same disregard. A minority of Diocesan Organ Advisors and freelance Organ Consultants were then historically and musically informed in their work. Regrettably, this was not the case of the Diocese of Bristol, which to this day is among the few who have yet to fully embrace the above values as they have burgeoned in the present-day society. It was not until a decade later that these values, already established in several European Countries led by the early 20th century example of Austria, followed by Australia (*Organ Historical Trust of Australia*) and the U.S.A. (*Organ Historical Society*), were consolidated in this country with the founding of *The British Institute of Organ Studies* (B.IO.S.) at an inaugural conference held at Queen's College, Cambridge in 1976. The Aims of B.I.O.S. are as follows:

To promote objective, scholarly research into the history of the organ and its music in all its aspects, and, in particular, into the organ and its music in Britain.

To conserve the sources and materials for the history of the organ in Britain, and make them accessible to scholars.

To work for the preservation, and where necessary the faithful restoration, of historic organs in Britain.

To encourage an exchange of scholarship with similar bodies and individuals abroad, and to promote a greater appreciation of historical overseas schools of organ-building.

In view of the above, it was doubly ironic given the fate that the inappropriate changes imposed on the organ of St Andrew's in 1965, that two years earlier, in the first edition of *The British Organ*, Cecil Clutton and Austin Niland wrote as follows:

'...Gray and Davison...made a number of extremely fine instruments of which very few survive in original condition. The Parish Churches at Chippenham, Wiltshire, and Usk, in Monmouthshire, are among the few survivors.'[157] Plates 37 and 38 taken by the author in 1964 show the Gray & Davison case and console shortly before their destruction.

Plate 37: The Gray and Davison South Case (author).

Plate 38: The Gray and Davison Console in 1964 (author).

Unfortunately, Clutton and Niland were then unaware of the initial work of Brice Seede, and of the changes made in 1931. When a revised second edition of their book appeared in 1982, not only had much of Gray & Davison's work at Chippenham had been destroyed, but a further incongruous intervention was not far away. Yet, the Gray & Davison organ at Usk, originally in Llandaff Cathedral, has had a happier outcome. Thanks to preliminary research and the fine craftsmanship of Nicholson & Co., this organ was faithfully restored to its original condition in 2005. Unlike Chippenham, which is a compromised *mélange* of Georgian and mid-Victorian pipework, Usk has an integral tonal style.

The general attitudes of the 1960s in British organ building encompassed a tendency to replace both mechanical and pneumatic actions with direct electric or electro-pneumatic systems. Detached consoles, laden with accessories to permit rapid changes of registration, became even more popular. Musically, there was an anti-Romantic tendency in favour of Neo-Classical designs for new instruments. It became fashionable to 'Baroquise' existing organs, replacing unfashionable Romanic timbres with new ranks of pipes, particularly mixtures, or to transpose or transfer pipes to achieve the desired or imagined effects. The Tierce rank in an English mixture stop such as the Sesquialtera was a frequent casualty which can be seen in the scheme proposed by J. W. Walker & Sons. (Appendix VI) Alternatively, fitting extension units which enabled several harmonic or mutation pitches to be derived from a single rank of pipes frequently resulted in musically insipid results.

The agenda for the rebuilding of the organ of St Andrew's reflected some of these tendencies: the incorporation of electro-pneumatic actions and of extension units operated remotely from a detached console. However, the gracefully cantilevered facade of the Gray & Davison chancel case and console were summarily destroyed, the void of the arch was filled by rank of 24 pipes a 16' bass extension to the Choir Organ Dulciana which resembled scaffolding. However, the input of architect Oswald Brakespear ensured that the Seede case facade was partially restored by removing inside the facade pipes added by Gray & Davison which had compromised its Classical symmetry.

In April 1961, Rushworth & Dreaper were invited to inspect the instrument and submit an estimate. The latter apparently became 'mislaid' by the Parish and the company provided a revised copy to Canon Snow in March 1963. (Appendix VII). Meanwhile, J.W. Walker & Son had previously submitted their estimate in November 1962 (Appendix VI).

Two years later, the Vicar reported to the Finance Committee that the organ was found to be in a very dangerous state and it was decided that it must be replaced [sic (meaning rebuilt?)] as soon as possible. It is likely that he had been most alarmed by the timber infestation reported by Rushworth & Dreaper. A sub-committee was convened comprising of The Vicar, Churchwardens and Mr. E.W. Minter (Treasurer), but curiously the Organist was excluded. The P.C.C. agreed that Vicar should approach the Trustees of the Stent Bequest. In addition, there was a reluctant agreement to make a public appeal following other unsatisfactory loan applications.

On 7th June 1963, following a £4,000 advance from the Stent Bequest, the Organ Sub-Committee agreed to award the contact to Percy Daniel & Co. of Clevedon and asked that the unsuccessful contenders (Rushworth & Dreaper and J.W.Walker & Sons Ltd.) be informed in writing. Daniels accepted the work and agreed to work in consultation with the church architect Oswald Brakespear.

Although both Rushworths and Daniels no longer exist, copies of the former's estimates of 1963 together with that of J.W.Walker & Sons are in the Parish Deposit at the Wiltshire History Centre.[158] Walker's estimate was the most detailed in endorsing the serious condition of the instrument, whilst Rushworth & Dreaper were especially preoccupied with the timber infestation. In other respects their estimate had much to commend it in that they were to retain the Gray & Davison chancel facade and console and would have been content to leave the 1879 specification virtually unaltered adding a Tremulant to the Swell which was originally proposed. However, their four optional estimates for extension units and other tonal changes to the Swell Organ would have been of little musical value. Their option to enclose the Choir Organ was again of limited musical facility.

The estimates of Walker and Daniel are not dissimilar in many aspects: each envisaged a new detached console and their enlarged specifications relied heavily on extensions from unit chests. Walker, unlike Rushworth or Daniel, were prepared to alter the compositions of the Great and Swell Mixtures and rename and/or transplant other ranks to give the instrument a Neo-Classical gloss. Most significantly, of the three contenders, it was only Walker's who realised the need to redesign the internal layout to give direct tonal projection into the Nave rather than across the Chancel. It was a very serious failing that this important point was not taken up by either of the Diocesan Organ Advisers, nor the church personnel.

Daniel's enlargements through unit chests are today of limited musical use, but it was commendable that the essential chorus of the Great Organ was not compromised, particularly as far as the two Mixtures were concerned. The transferring of the Choir Clarinet to the Swell Organ was most regrettable in that it prevents the prescribed registrations of much of the English and French repertoires through almost three centuries to be correctly registered. Before his opening recital Dr. Douglas Fox was heard to remark: 'whose silly idea was that!'

The input of Mr Oswald Brakespear (the church's architect from 1946 until 1990) was significant especially in view of his recognition of the potential of restoring the Seede case to some semblance of its former glory by moving inside the overflow facade pipes that Gray & Davison had added [159] inside the instrument. His remarks on the organ case in his 1961 quinquennial inspection were as follows:[160]

'1961 March...On the west it retains a splendid late seventeenth or early eighteenth century oak case in need of cleaning but apparently sound. The pipes elaborately stencilled in the last century should be repainted or gilded when this is done.'

This historically correct and aesthetically tasteful advice was ignored by the Parish and was to be ignored again in his report on work carried out in the 1980s (see below). Thus the finest piece of Georgian furniture in the area remains to this day darkly stained, with the dull zinc facade pipes exuding an air of repressive dullness. Some impressions of the original waxed light oak finish are evident in areas which were beyond the reach of the varnisher's brush. The Photomontage of the case which features in this monograph gives the reader an impression of the potential for an historically informed restoration as was recommended by Oswald Brakespear.

A meeting was held between Daniels, Brakespear and John Tomlins in August 1963. Some small alterations were made to the specification but these were accommodated within the £6,000 budget. It was agreed that work would begin on this extravagant rebuild by Easter 1964 as follows:

SPECIFICATION AND ESTIMATE FOR REBUILDING, MODERNISATION AND ELECTRIFICATION OF THE ORGAN, INCORPORATING THE BEST OF THE OLD PIPEWORK AND OTHER MATERIAL

Compass of Manuals CC to C 61 notes

Compass of Pedals CCC to f1 32 notes

GREAT ORGAN

1. Double Diapason Old 16ft.

2. Open Diapason No.1 Old 8ft. new from T.C. up

3. Open Diapason No.2 Old 8ft.

4. Clarabella Old 8ft

5. Principal Old 4ft.

6. Harmonic Flute Old 4ft.

7. Twelfth Old 2 2/3 ft.

8. Fifteenth Old 2ft.

9. Sesquialtera Old III rks.

10. Fourniture (19-22) Old II rks.

11. Trumpet Old 8ft. revoiced

12. Clarion Old 4ft. revoiced

SWELL ORGAN

13. Open Diapason Old 8ft.

14. Stopped Diapason Old 8ft.

15. Gamba T.C. new 8ft. grooved bass

16. Voix Celeste T.C new 8ft.

17. Principal Old 4ft.

18. Rohr Flute New 4ft.

19. Fifteenth Old 2 ft.

20. Mixture (19-22-26) Old, remodelled. III Rks.

21. Oboe new bass 16ft. unit, treble revoiced

22. Oboe Old 8ft.

23. Cornopean Old 8 ft. revoiced

24. Clarion Old 4 ft. revoiced

CHOIR ORGAN

25. Double Dulciana New 16ft.

26. Viol da Gamba Old 8ft.

27. Stopped Diapason Old 8ft.

28. Dulciana Old 8ft.

29. Gemshorn Old 4ft.

30. Flute Old 4ft.

31. Dulcet extension from No.29 4ft.

32. Nazard New 2 2/3 ft.

33. Piccolo Old 2ft

34. Tierce New 1 3/5 ft.

35. Larigot extension from No.29 1 1/3ft.

36. Superoctave

PEDAL ORGAN

37. Contra Bourdon 32ft. Lowest 7 Acoustic [sic], quint notes [of] old Swell Double Diapason re-named

38. Open Diapason Wood Old 16ft.

39. Open Diapason Metal Old 16ft. From Great Double Diapason

40. Bourdon Old 16ft. Stopped Diapason renamed

41. Dulciana 16ft. From Choir No.25

42. Bass Flute 8ft. From No. 40

43. Violoncello Old 8ft.

44 . Octave Quint 5 1/3ft. From No.36

45. Oboe 16 ft. From Swell No. 21.

46. Trombone Old 16 ft.

COUPLERS

47. Choir to Pedal

48. Great to Pedal

49. Swell to Pedal

50. Swell to Great

51. Swell to Choir

52. Choir to Great

53. Swell Octave

54. Swell Sub-Octave

55. Swell Unison off

56. Great and Pedal Combinations Coupled.

ACCESSORIES

6 thumb pistons to Great.

6 thumb pistons to Swell.

6 thumb pistons to Choir.

6 toe pistons to Pedal.

Five toe pistons to Swell (duplicating thumb pistons).

1 thumb reverser Great to Pedal.

1 toe reverser for Great to Pedal.

1 thumb reverser Swell to Great.

Pistons adjustable from a setter board in the console.

'Discus' blower.

DETACHED CONSOLE

Musically, the outcome of this rebuild was not flawless and did not justify the cost. The revoicing of the reeds was disappointing and left them devoid of the brightness characteristic of Gray & Davison. [161] The weak tone and slow speech of the Pedal Trombone remains a musical handicap. The stops of the extension units of the Choir and Pedal Organs were tonally weak and of limited utility. Their locations particularly those of the Pedal Organ are very cramped. The detached console resulted in a slight time lag in the response of the new electro-pneumatic actions. Nevertheless, the tone of the Seede and Gray & Davison flue ranks remained relatively uncompromised.

The Rededication was held at Evensong on 28th February, 1965 and was attended by the present writer. The input of the choir included the Introit 'O Come ye servants of the Lord' by Tye, and Stanford's anthem: ' I saw another angel ascending from the east.' 'The Old Hundredth' was sung to an unpublished arrangement for organ, trumpets and drums by Sir Edward Bairstow. The concluding voluntary was a performance of J.S.Bach's Prelude in B minor (B.W.V. 544) pro organo pleno but registered in a manner that was far from the 'full organ' direction on the composer's holograph. In order to demonstrate the new array of registration aids it began quietly on the Great flutes and there was gradual 'build- up' to full organ. Such was the fashion amongst many English organists of the time. The detached console and the infill of the chancel arch with a bass rank of Dulciana pipes are illustrated in Plates 33-41. The rededication was also marked by an organ recital by Dr. Douglas Fox, who had tragically lost an arm during military service. His programme included J.S.Bach's Fugue in G (B.W.V. 577) and an arrangement of Debussy's Cantata 'The Blessed Damozel'. This was followed by a performance of Mozart's Requiem Mass (K.626) by members of various Chippenham church choirs with an organ accompaniment played by John Tomlins.

Plate 39: The 1965 detached console, uncluttered by the equipment currently required to overcome problems of communication arising from the Nave Altar and experimental relocations of the choir.

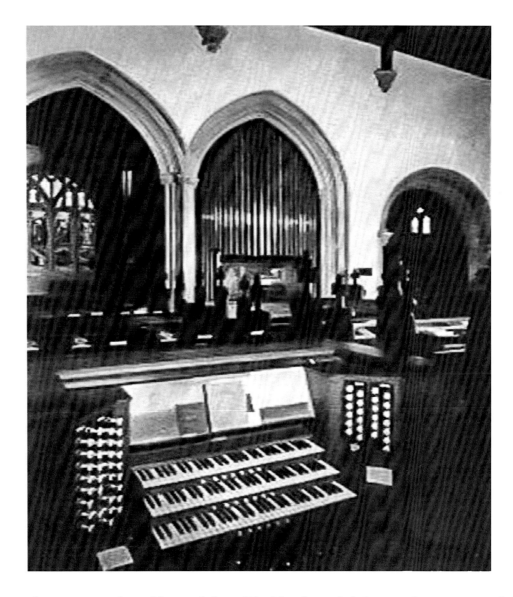

Plate 40: the 1965 console and beyond the infill of the discarded Gray and Davison South façade case and console with a 16' bass extension to the choir organ Dulciana, the latter being removed 20 years later.

The Finance Committee Minutes provide a concise summary of the next decade.[162] By 1970 there were the first discussions of partial reordering and the institution of a Nave Altar. The Organ Fund had been continued and stood at £82.5.10 on 12th November. On 15th April 1971 an increase of the organist's salary of £210 p.a. was discussed and again in 1973, but it remained frozen. During the 1973 dry summer, Philip Snow suggested £200 for an organ humidifier, but the weather moderated and all was well.

John Tomlins retired in March 1982, and the post was advertised at £600-£700 p.a. His successor, Peter Jezard, was appointed at £650 p.a. in the following October. During the interim period the author and John Nourse served as deputies.

The Late Twentieth Century

On 10th November 1983 Jezard requested four tunings a year from Daniels[163] to which the Finance Committee agreed. Meanwhile, he had been in touch with a Robin Winn (an organ builder of uncertain credentials) then working in the area. Jezard expressed reservations about the nature of Daniel's work and costs in an undated letter to the Finance Committee as follows:

'I would like to propose, for the consideration of the Finance Committee, that we change the tuning contract and place the work in the hands of Mr. Robin Winn of Melksham, I know Mr. Winn personally and can vouch for his high level of skill as a craftsman; "*Werkprinzip*" philosophy of the eighteenth century is his speciality which of course is the most appropriate for the preservation of the tonal structure of the instrument...'[164]

This appraisal was far from the truth, Winn was not professionally accredited, and his track record less than satisfactory in several areas of the country. It was grossly incorrect to relate the North European Renaissance/Baroque Werkprinzip philosophy as an appropriate style for an English organ that is a fusion of our eighteenth and mid-nineteenth century styles.

Meanwhile, Percy Daniel & Co. wrote to the Churchwarden, Michael Hathaway agreeing on 13th December to tune the organ quarterly. They also reminded the church that the twenty-five year guarantee on the work completed in 1965 would expire in 1990 provided that the instrument remained in their care for routine tuning, cleaning and servicing.

No doubt, arising from the introduction of a nave altar and the various experimental relocations of the choir on the north and south sides of the nave adjacent to it, Daniels had also been asked to report on a relocation of the console in these two Nave positions. The company reported that the existing cables from the detached console in the chancel were of insufficient length to reach the positions suggested and would have to be replaced. They explained that the work would entail removing flagstones to create ducts both for the action cables and the swell pedal. They also suggested that if the north side were preferred the console would be better sunk into a pit as at present. Their estimate for this work was £2,000 - £2,200 plus V.A.T.[165] No further action was taken by the P.C.C. on this issue which left the organist 'flying blind' in relation to the choir. [166] In his Quinquennial Report of 1984, Oswald Brakespear repeated his earlier advice that:

'Consideration should one day be given to gilding parts of this splendid organ case.'

Although there is no extant supporting documentation, it would appear that Messrs. Jezard and Winn, presumably with the consent of the Vicar (the Revd. Michael Taylor), planned an alternative scheme, which was to have unsatisfactory musical and aesthetic consequences. On 23rd May 1985 the P.C.C. accepted a recommendation of the Church Music and Concerts Committee that the 'old pipes [in fact these were those of the 1965 16ft. Dulciana rank filling the gap created by the destruction of the Gray & Davison Chancel facade and console] should be sold for £200; the money going towards the purchase of a new Trumpet stop for the organ at a cost of £350 plus the £200 for the old [sic] pipes.'

However, the Trumpet stop was certainly not new, Winn supplied a second hand rank from a redundant organ by Conacher. Nevertheless, on 14th November 1985 it was agreed that the Vicar and Mr. Jezard obtain quotations for the cleaning and renovation of the organ. On January 16th

1986 Jezard, was asked to proceed with quotations for this work. 'An account of £300 was passed for the Trumpet Major.' [sic] On 15th May 1986 the PCC discussed quotations for organ renovation and cleaning.

At this point, the *British Institute of Organ Studies* expressed serious concern through a letter to the Vicar from the founding Secretary: Dr. Nicholas Thistlethwaite. The Vicar conceded that the estimate of John Coulson of Bristol be accepted, when we see our way clear to finance the project.'[167] The Vicar also conceded that work of this nature to an historic instrument should not have been embarked upon without a D.A.C. Faculty obtained after consulting the Diocesan Organ Adviser, Canon John Bradley. The Parish then applied for a 'Faculty for Renovation' on 16th October 1986.

The Diocesan Chancellor's Faculty Certificate was duly issued and on 10th February 1987 the P.C.C. launched an appeal to the congregation for funds.168 On 19th March an initial payment of £800 towards Coulson's estimate of £5,259 was authorised and paid on 9th April. By May 1987 a further £1,166-90 had been raised.

In consultation with Oswald Brakespear, it was agreed to use some panels of the oak returns of the 1752 case (but see below), which had been stored inside the instrument to partially fill the lower part of the void on the Chancel side of the instrument that had been created by the removal of the Dulciana pipes mentioned above. Brakespear also advised that the space above the panels be filled with a rank of non-speaking pipes. This was not only an aesthetic recommendation but one of security, but the parish again foolishly ignored this advice.

The Vicar informed the PCC that this protective panelling would cost no more than £800 (plus V.A.T.), but by 19th September this had risen to £1,500. Here again the P.C.C. minutes are contradicted by the Archives: an invoice from a joiner, R.Weston of Corsham, describes the 'Supply of purpose made oak panelling, framing, mouldings etc. Tone to match the existing doors.' Thus, it was only these doors that had formed part of the 1752 case.

During the spring and summer of 1987, whilst the instrument was dismantled, the author, with the permission of John Coulson and the Parish, was able to carry out a detailed study of the original 1752 pipework and assess how it might best relate to the 1879 rebuilding of the instrument by Gray and Davison in the future, should suitably enlightened attitudes prevail. The results were published in the *Journal of the British Institute of Organ Studies*.[169]

By 12th November 1987 only half of the £8,000 required had been raised and a target date of 31st January 1988 set as the closing date for further donations. Coulson completed the work on 11th February 1988; a total of £3,365.58 had been raised by the congregation.

It was agreed on 10th March to retain 10% of Coulson's account for 6 months and the remaining balance was paid on 14th April. In June 1988 a five year contract was concluded with Coulson for tuning and maintenance, ie. until 1993.

In his next Quinquennial Report, Oswald Brakespear noted in July 1989 that the Organ had been rebuilt [sic] since the last inspection and some old doors and new panelling to match them fitted on the south side. He was critical of the alterations to the Chancel façade particularly that his advice regarding the filling of the void above the new panelling with dummy facade pipes:

'The pipes which it was understood have not been fitted. Without them, the exposed [internal] pipes of the organ look more useful than ornamental.'[170]

Coulson's work of 'restoration of the voicing,' as far as the Great reeds were concerned was a partial improvement on the work of Daniel's in 1965. However, the 'restoration of the voicing' of the rest of the Great Organ was unsatisfactory. Pieces of paving stone were placed on the latter's reservoir in order to increase the tonal projection from the chamber. This expedient increased the wind pressure of the Great Organ to a level at which the Mixture ranks screamed stridently. This was rectified at the suggestion of the present writer by Roger Taylor, when the care of the organ was transferred to Nicholson & Co. A remaining problem is the underwinding of the Pedal Organ. The wind supply to the recycled Trumpet stop (initially fitted by Winn and Jezard 'as an experiment') is ducted from the Pedal Organ reservoir. This has created further tonal weaknesses in the four main pedal stops, which are located at the rear of the chamber, which is also an impediment to their tonal projection.

The organ chamber roof sustained storm damage yet again in September 1990, and repairs by Downing, Rudman & Bent were covered by insurance. Almost a year later Jezard reported that the unprotected area above the panelling of the Chancel facade had allowed unauthorised access to the interior of the organ, allegedly by school children. This resulted in damage to a number of pipes. Such was the consequence of ignoring the prudent advice of the Architect referred to above. Coulson recommended that a metal grille be fitted into the opening, which was authorised and duly installed in September 1991. A necessary precaution, but this currently remains an aesthetic eyesore (Plate 41).

Plate 41: The current unprepossessing south face of the instrument in the former chancel.

In 1998 and 1999 Ian Bell, formerly of N.P.Mander Ltd., was engaged to examine the instrument in the role of an independent adviser. He prepared a discussion document rather than a working schedule in which he stressed that:

'The report does not attempt to study or consider further the detailed history of the instrument, which has already been the subject of concentrated research and several published papers by Dr. Christopher Kent. His conclusions are accepted, and are not brought into question by anything that I have seen within the organ myself.'[171]

Bell was overtly critical of the work carried out in the 1980s when some unfortunate tonal tinkering took place, begun by Robin Winn, an unaccredited organ builder, and completed by John Coulson of Bristol. This included the addition of a second-hand Trumpet rank, using the stop knobs originally allocated to the 16-foot Dulciana, the pipes of which were accordingly removed. Various ranks were 'revoiced' on site, in an operation which might, in that respect, be fairly said to be a doubtful use of good money. [172]

In 1984, the present writer concluded the second edition of a monograph on the instrument[173] as follows:

'Traditions of worship in the closing decades of this century are becoming orientated to the nave in order to permit maximum congregational participation. In view of this it seems most logical to predict that the next phase in the history of this organ will be its restoration to the original west gallery position of 1752. From here it will speak clearly and articulately in both service and concert use'

Ian Bell[174] drew a similar conclusion in his report of 1999. After discussing the complexities created by the current location and various other options he was to conclude the 'Best of all would be the most acoustically efficient position, centrally at one end or the other of the nave.....or by placing the organ at the West end either free standing on the floor, with the choir on either side, or on a free-standing gallery on four wooden columns, forward of the entrance.'

To summarise the matter economically, Bell noted that the twentieth century has seen more than one 'doubtful use of good money' by the parish. The instrument's original tracker action had functioned from 1752 to at least 1868, that of 1879 for a further half-century. Yet the twentieth century was to see the economic domino effect of two changes to non-mechanical actions. First, the cheapest pneumatic action, which had a life span of just over thirty years; second, an electro-pneumatic system which is now receiving remedial repairs and replacements of components as required. The inappropriate location of the organ in relation to the nave altar and the experiments with choir locations were also singled out for criticism in a study by Martin Freke of 2005.[175]

The 21st Century and The St Andrew's Project.

The new millennium also began badly. In 2003, an integral part of the ill-fated 'St. Andrew's Project' was to be the relocation of the organ into a new West Gallery which would stand forward of a Narthex and also incorporate catering facilities and lavatories beneath. At the initiative of the Revd. Simon Tatton-Brown (Vicar 2000-2013) this inspired reordering project was to include a restoration of the organ in a new West Gallery, returning it to mechanical actions and consolidating the remaining Seede and Gray & Davison pipework. The present writer was invited to join the planning committee as the organ consultant. The examination of the pipework conducted in 1987[176] shaped the following proposed west gallery specification in 2003:

Compasses: Ped., Gt. and Ch: GG/AA - a³; Sw. CC-a³; Ped. CC- f1

Couplers: Gt.-Ped, Sw-Ped, Sw-Gt., Sw.- Ch.

Four mechanical composition pedals to Gt., Ped., and Sw.

Tremulant.

Straight and concave pedalboard.

Great Organ	Choir Organ.
Open Diapason 8	Stopped Diapason 8*
Stopped Diapason 8*	Flute 4*
Principal (in halves) 4*	Principal 4*
Flute 4*	Cremona 8*
Twelfth 2 2/3	
Fifteenth 2	Swell Organ.
Sesquialtera 17.19.22	Open Diapason 8
Fourniture III	Stopped Diapason 8
Cornet V	Gamba 8
Trumpet (in halves) 8	Principal 4
Cremona 8*	Fifteenth 2
	Cornet II
Pedal Organ.	Hautboy 8
Open Wood 16	Trumpet 8
Bourdon 16	
Principal 8	
Trombone 16	

This scheme received the support of organ builders including Goetze & Gwynn Ltd. (Appendix VII1), William Drake (Appendix IX), Peter Collins (Appendix X) and Nicholson & Co. The proposal was also endorsed by the Organ Adviser to the Diocesan Advisory Committee, and the proposals for the organ were further submitted to the present writer's colleagues for peer review. Their responses, together with the report following a visit from the Advisory Committee of the Council for the Care of Churches (now the *Church Buildings Council*), were as follows:

'Dear Mr. Tatton-Brown,
Chippenham, St Andrew (Diocese of Bristol): Proposed rebuilding of organ and other works.

Thank you for making Dr. Berrow, Mr. Lamb and I welcome when we visited Chippenham on 3 December to discuss the proposals for rebuilding the organ and other works. This was discussed by the Council at its meeting on 26 January and I write now with its advice.

The Council's delegation was met by the incumbent, the Revd. Simon Tatton-Brown, Mr. Davies, organist, Mr. Mann, a member of Bristol DAC and Dr. Kent, consultant for the organ scheme. Although Dr. Kent is a member of the Council's Organs Committee his views were not canvassed by the Council. I am glad to be able to tell you that the Council generally supported your proposals and overall approach to your needs in the building. It understands in particular that the proposals for the organ are good.

However, it made a number of detailed comments which it hoped the parish will take on board. The Council noted that church has an extremely fine oak organ case, which is one of two examples extant of a west-country pattern of eighteenth-century cases. It is presently in the north transept of the church where its glory cannot be appreciated. It contains an organ that was most recently overhauled and partly revoiced by John Coulson in 1987 but which incorporates the significant Seede pipes from 1752 and others by Gray & Davison, 1879. This pre-twentieth century material is being used for a proposed new organ in the existing case to be built on a new west gallery, according to the proposals of Goetze & Gwynn. The historic elements of the organ case will be restored by Penny's Mill Designs according to their specification.

The Council understands that the proposed new organ draws heavily on the English eighteenth-century tradition, the date of the core of the surviving historic pipework in the present instrument. It also incorporates elements of the Gray & Davison addition to the organ in 1879, most especially in the downwards extension of the Swell compass and the Pedal organ. With the exception of the Great Cremona and Pedal Principal (both new stops) the organ will incorporate varying amounts of historic pipework in each rank. The organ will have an entirely new action, winding and chests. The most recent unsatisfactory additions to the organ will be lost. It is unlikely that they are of particular significance. However, it would be useful for it to be clearly stated in the proposals what, if any, historic material will be put aside. There is an unresolved discussion in the proposal about the Pedal Open Wood, 16', which is presently not satisfactory. The Council hopes that this stop will survive provided it can be accommodated in the new gallery. The Council would advise in favour of this high-quality scheme.

The Council noted that the proposals for the organ case from Penny's Mill designs suggest that their work will be limited to consolidation of any weak areas of the existing structure, replacing missing elements and refinishing. Photographic and written documentation will be provided. The finish of the case would ideally be close to its original colour, but no rationale is provided for the basis of identifying this. The Council accepts the principle behind this work but advises that a drawing is prepared of the case as it stands indicating where missing elements will be replaced and any structural repairs to be done and that the finish of the case is agreed with the conservators.

The Council agrees that the proposal to site the organ on a new gallery at the west end of the church is entirely appropriate and understandable and that it will see the organ returned to an earlier location…The gallery could, for example, have fielded panels in traditional Georgian design and be of sufficient size to contain the organ and a group of singers or other musicians…..

Yours sincerely.
David Knight.
Conservation Assistant.

Notwithstanding the flawless aesthetic perception of the plans, other factors led to its failure. These included extensive roof repairs which were soon to be followed by major work to the tower and the failure to commission professional fund-raising plans for the Organ Gallery and Narthex facilities. The outcome of an open congregation meeting held in April 2005 was little short of devastating for the immediate prospect of the organ being returned to a West Gallery location. Only a few of those present were prepared to offer their support, notwithstanding the approvals of the scheme that had been expressed by members of the Organ Committee of the Archbishop's *Church Buildings Council* and the Association of Independent Organ Advisers. Further support followed in a letter of 17th September to the Vicar from the Chairman of the Birmingham Diocesan Advisory Committee and member of *The Cathedrals Commission*, Dr. James Berrow:

'...It was my privilege to visit the church in 2005, on behalf of the Council for the Care of Churches and offer advice on the existing instrument and planned restoration. In essence, this was to secure the future of the outstanding mid-eighteenth century case and return it to its original role, containing an appropriate instrument, ideally on a west gallery but, possibly, on the floor of the church in a freestanding position. At present it is poorly sited and, though many rebuilds, organ builders have endeavoured to achieve sufficient power to overcome its location, rather than restore the organ to its intended position. The case has become nothing more than a façade, concealing an instrument which has grown in a rather haphazard way and, hence, has lost its musical integrity.'

An historically informed restorations of the superb Seede case and the best of the nineteenth-century material would prove a magnet to future musicians and may attract heritage grant-aid. It certainly represents the best value for a long-term solution to St. Andrew's musical life...' [177]

The project also attracted positive support from the international historically informed musicological community as may be seen in the letters that comprise Appendix XIV, from which the following is an example:

'From: Dr. Barbara Owen, Newburyport, Mass., U.S.A.

Past President of the Organ Historical Society, Past Regional Councillor and Chapter Dean of the American Guild of Organists, recipient of the Curt Sachs award of the American Musical Instrument Society, and an independent organ consultant who has engaged in projects with over eighty churches and other organizations in the United States, including several involving organs of historical significance.

A few years ago, in company with Dr. Christopher Kent, I visited the Chippenham Parish Church, and saw for the first time the organ there. My first impression was something akin to "how are the mighty fallen." Here was the shade of a once splendid organ, a masterwork of an important regional builder, now ineffectively "modernized" both tonally and mechanically. Its elegant Georgian casework, once the centrepiece of the west gallery, had also been altered, and awkwardly crammed into an unsuitable space in the north aisle, where it not only cannot be seen to advantage, but also detracts from the symmetry of the focal point of the room. At that time, we discussed how splendid it would be if this organ could be sympathetically restored to its former musical and visual elegance - as well as to its very functional purpose of effectively leading congregational song from its original location in the west gallery. To do so would also restore the chancel area to its original more open and symmetrical appearance.

Now I am informed that a plan has been drawn up to accomplish these admirable ends. As I read through it, my enthusiasm for the project mounted. Over the years, I have seen (and occasionally had the good fortune to be involved in) a number of similar projects successfully carried out, in England, Australia, on the Continent, and in the United States. In every instance, these projects have not only focused the attention of the musical and historical public on the church, but in many cases also to have assisted in revitalising congregational life and enhancing the civic pride of the community. Indeed, a frequent by-product of many a worthy organ restoration project has been to attract a good competent church musician who has brought new life to a church's musical offerings, both liturgically and through secular concerts.

I thus thoroughly endorse the well-thought-out rebuilding/restoration plan for the organ now proposed by Dr. Kent - who, as performer, historian, and independent consultant, is eminently qualified for the task. While it is perhaps not always easy for the lay person to grasp the musical and aesthetic ramifications inherent in the successful outcome of such an undertaking, they immediately become clear upon its completion. I for one look forward to a future visit to Chippenham if this excellent plan can be properly implemented, and am quite certain that I am not alone in this.

Barbara Owen, Ph.D., M.M., Ch.M.'

It was unfortunate, but essential, that the architect recommended extensive repairs to both the roofs and tower which have of necessity taken priority over any immediate plans for the St Andrew's Project's historically informed restoration of the organ and relocation to a West Gallery. So for the foreseeable future the organ is likely to remain in its stifling chamber and remain serviceable with the support of a make-do and mend ethos through the capable hands of Nicholson & Co: In 2010 the Great Organ key-contacts were178 replaced, and in 2012 the pedal board was completely overhauled and the key-contacts similarly renewed. This has gone some way towards alleviating the disembodied time lag that the player experiences between depressing keys and the speech of the pipes.

Previously, in 2008, the damage sustained by the carved panels of the case in order to accommodate the additional Trumpet, was conserved and repaired by Penny's Mills of Bedwyn with the support of an anonymous donor. Meanwhile, the finest surviving item of mid-Georgian organ furniture in the South West of England serves as a convenient location to hang fire extinguishers (Plate 42) and the space in front of the façade serves from time to time as a stacking area for chairs. The recurring timber infestation of the softwood outer panels, notwithstanding treatment, continues to be a cause for concern.

The elegant panelling of the 1965 detached console so carefully designed by Oswald Brakespear has of late acquired an accumulation of electronic aids and devices, visually helpful to organists given the location of the choir, but less than attractive in appearance.

Latterly, well-designed and tidily constructed catering facilities and an obtrusive lavatory

Plate 42: A Fire extinguisher intensively attached to the South return of the Seede case.

enclosure cabinet has been built along the wall of the north aisle. Although eminently practical they are limited in their aesthetic appeal and do not accord with the architecture of the church.

𝕿𝖍𝖊 𝕱𝖚𝖙𝖚𝖗𝖊?

It is commendable that the church has begun a programme of essential repairs to the life- expired 1965 electric actions, and damage to the Great soundboard from rainwater. Hopefully, this will not recur now that the roof of the chamber has been extensively repaired. There remain larger questions which have yet to be satisfactorily addressed. First, the unsatisfactory position and interior layout of the instrument to permit optimum sound projection into the Nave and ease of accessibility for tuning and maintenance. Attention has been drawn to this in several previous reports: namely, Arthur Harrison in 1915, J. W. Walker & Sons in 1964, the present author since 1973, and by Ian Bell in 1997/99.

Second, the casework: in 1965 Oswald Brakespear oversaw the removal of the 1879 diapering from the facade pipes of the 1752 case and recommended that they be gilded in the C18th manner. He was to repeat this advice at several Quinquennial inspections through to his retirement in 1989. The aesthetic prospect of the south side of the organ also leaves much to be desired. This is the result of work completed by the late John Coulson in 1989.

It would be inappropriate to conclude without mentioning the organ of the Prytanée in La Flèche, Chippenham's twin town in France. There also is an historic instrument, which dates from both the seventeenth and eighteenth centuries which also has endured many alterations. In 1996 an historically based restoration and reconstruction were completed. The outcome of this work has been aptly proclaimed by the French virtuoso André Isoir as 'a resurrection.' This organ has recently been recorded by Dr. David Ponsford, whose recital at St. Andrew's in May 2013 employed deft registrations of great finesse which shed further light on the latent tonal qualities currently 'locked in' to the instrument by its poor location and life-expired electric actions.[173]

The photomontage of the organ restored within the Seede case, as it would appear relocated in a West Gallery features as both the frontispiece and end plate. This fine Georgian case deemed by Canon Philip Snow as 'the finest treasure of this church' and the identification of much contemporaneous pipework is fully deserving of a restoration which will return it to its original 'place of honour' with an *en fenetre* console with mechanical key and stop actions. It is significant to note that the Church Buildings Council Organ Advisory Committee and the Diocesan Advisory Committee were positively disposed towards such a scheme of restoration as planned in 2003.

In conclusion, it is to be hoped that future generations may follow the examples of our European twin towns of La Flèche and Friedberg in the faithful restorations their historic organs. Therefore, I trust that the foregoing may be of some relevance to this end in the future. Although it is currently difficult to be optimistic.

Explicit.

Appendix I

Dimensions of the Brice Seede Case:
Impost width 12'
Depth from scale drawing of 1787: 7' 6"
Console overhang at the centre of the Impost 5'
Central tower width 5'
Central tower height 10'
Pipe field widths within central tower: 3' centre 1' outer.
Outer tower heights above impost 8'.
Outer tower widths 1'.

Behind the façade at the bases of the central tower and flats are holes which originally received the lead tubes which conveyed air to the gilded speaking pipes. The holes indicate that 17 pipes were winded forming the bass register of the Great Organ Open Diapason (GG/AA /Bb - tenor c.)

Appendix II: Harrison & Harrison 1915 Proposal and Estimate.

(Those ranks marked * are likely to have been reused from 'the old organ.')

PEDAL ORGAN, 7 stops, 3 Couplers [CC - f1]

		PIPES	NOTES
1. SUB BORDUN	32	Wood	30
2. OPEN WOOD*	16	Wood	30
3. GEIGEN (from Great)	16	Metal	30
4. SUB BASS*	16	Wood	30
5. OCTAVE WOOD (10 from No.2)	8	Wood	12
6. FLUTE (18 from No. 4)	8	Wood	30
7. OPHICLEIDE	16	Metal	30

I. CHOIR TO PEDAL
II. GREAT TO PEDAL
III. SWELL TO PEDAL

CHOIR ORGAN, 7 stops, 1 coupler

8. LIEBLICH BORDUN	16	Wood	58
9. GEMSHORN*	8	Wood	58
10. STOPPED DIAPASON *	8	Wood	58
11. VIOLA DA GAMBA	8	Metal	58
12. WALD FLUTE	4	Wood	58
13. PICCOLO*	2	Metal	58
14. CLARINET	8	Metal	58

IV SWELL TO CHOIR

GREAT ORGAN 12 Stops, 2 Couplers.

15. GROSS GEIGEN	16	Metal	58
16. LARGE OPEN DIAPASON	8	Metal	58
17. SMALL OPEN DIAPASON*	8	Metal	58
18. GAMBA	8	Metal	58
19. CLARIBEL FLUTE*	8	Wood	58
20. OCTAVE *	4	Metal	58
21. HARMONIC FLUTE*	4	Metal	58
22. OCTAVE QUINT*	2 2/3	Metal	58

23. SUPER OCTAVE*	2	Metal	58
24. SESQUIALTERA 17.19.22*	III	Metal	174
25. TROMBA (harmonic trebles)	8	Metal	58
26. OCTAVE TROMBA (harmonic trebles)	4	Metal	58
V. CHOIR TO GREAT			
VI. SWELL TO GREAT			

SWELL ORGAN 11 STOPS, Tremulant & 1 coupler.

27 . OPEN DIAPASON	8	Metal	58
28. LIEBLICH GEDECKT*?	8	Metal	58
29. SALICIONAL	8	Metal	58
30. VOX ANGELICA (ten.c)	8	Metal	58
31. PRINCIPAL	4	Metal	58
32. FIFTEENTH	2	Metal	58
33. MIXTURE* 19.22.26.29	IV	Metal	232
VII. TREMULANT			
34. DOUBLE TRUMPET	16	Metal	58
35. TRUMPET (harmonic trebles)	8	Metal	58
36. CLARION (harmonic trebles)	4	Metal	58
VIII. OCTAVE			

ACCESSORIES

Four combination pedals to the Pedal Organ.
Three combination pedals to the Choir Organ.
Five combination pedals to the Great Organ.
Five combination pedals to the Swell Organ.
Reversible pedal to Great to Pedal.
Reversible piston Swell to Great.
Reversible piston to Tremulant.

WIND PRESSURES

Pedal flue-work 4 1/2", reeds 9".
Choir 2 1/2"
Great flue-work 4 , reeds 9"
Swell flue-work & Oboe 3 1/2", reeds 9"
Action 9"
The pedal-board to be radiating and concave and each key to be faced with hard teak.

The drawstop jambs to be set at an angle of 45 degrees to the keyboards the stop knobs to have solid ivory fronts. The speaking stops to be lettered in black and the couplers in red. The couplers to be grouped with the speaking stops to the organ they augment.

The whole organ to be reconstructed and rebuilt on a new main frame as a new instrument. The best portions of the present organ to be carefully restored and preserved. The pipe-work utilised again to be thoroughly cleaned and restored, transposed and where necessary re-scaled and revoiced with new pipes added in the bass.

The organ to be tuned to the new French pitch i.e. c [2] = 517 vibrations at 60 degrees F.

The blowing apparatus is not included in this estimate. The printed "Particulars of Construction" overleaf will apply except where they differ from the written particular heretofore when the written particulars are to prevail.

FOURTEEN HUNDRED AND EIGHTY-FIVE POUNDS

and the OLD ORGAN

28th October [19]15   E. Douglas Taylor, Esq..

APPENDIX III

E.Douglas Taylor, Esq./Chippenham 15th Nov. 1915.

Dear Mr. Taylor,

The Parish Church

I have just returned to Durham after nearly a fortnight's absence, and can now reply to your letter of Oct. 28th.

The Gamba could be changed for a Hohl Flöte if you would like it better; but, if this change were made the Claribel Flute should be transferred to the Choir and the Stopped Diapason to the Great. Otherwise there would be two open wood unenclosed 8ft. stops on the Great, which is not advisable on the grounds of variety.

The undulating stop on the Swell could not be a Viole unless a still keener toned Viole were substituted for the Salicional. There would be a keen-toned stop on the Choir, viz. the Viola da Gamba, which would be an entirely new stop of the modern type, and I think the choir is the better place for it. It would tend to greater variety if the Salicional were retained on the Swell. However, please think this over and we can discuss it again.

As regards a Lieblich Bordun 16ft. on the Swell, I think this stop can be done without. It is far more important that there should be a double flue of this character on the Choir. The first 16ft. in the Swell ought always to be a reed, and you would have it in the Double Trumpet. You will find in many of our up-to-date schemes, some larger than this one, that the Swell has no flue double. It is quite an unimportant stop for accompanimental purposes, and the "Full Swell" effect is dependent on the reeds and mixtures and in the Swell ensemble the foundation flue-work should if anything be subservient to the reeds. / Has your Church Council yet met and decided anything?/ With kind regards/ Yours very truly; Arthur Harrison.

Appendix IV: Harrison & Harrison 1931 Estimates.

Scheme I (Those ranks marked * are likely to have been reused from 'the old organ.')

PEDAL ORGAN, 6 Stops, 3 Couplers [CC-f1]

1. OPEN WOOD*	16	Wood.
2. SUB BASS	16	Wood.
3. GEIGEN	16 (from No.14)	Metal.
4. OCTAVE WOOD	8 (18 from No.1)	Wood.
5. FLUTE	8 (18 from No.2)	Wood.
6. OPHICLEIDE	16	Metal.

I CHOIR TO PEDAL
II GREAT TO PEDAL
III SWELL TO PEDAL

CHOIR ORGAN 7 stops, 1 Coupler (in a swell-box)

7. LIEBLICH BOURDON	16	Wood.
8. GEMSHORN	8	Metal.
9. STOPPED DIAPASON*	8	Wood.
10. VIOLA DA GAMBA*	8	Metal.
11. WALD FLUTE	4	Wood.
12. PICCOLO*	2	Metal.
13. CLARINET*	8	Metal.

IV SWELL TO CHOIR.

GREAT ORGAN. 12 Stops, 2 Couplers.

14. DOUBLE GEIGEN	16	Metal.
15. LARGE OPEN DIAPASON	8	Metal.
16. SMALL OPEN DIAPASON*	8	Wood and Metal.
17. GEIGEN	8	Metal.
18. CLARIBEL FLUTE*	8	Wood.
19. OCTAVE	4	Metal.
20. HARMONIC FLUTE*	4	Metal.
21. OCTAVE QUINT	2 2/3	Metal.
22. SUPER OCTAVE	2	Metal.
23. HARMONICS	17, 19, 21, 22	Metal.
24. TROMBA (Harmonic Trebles)	8	Metal.
25. OCTAVE TROMBA	4	Metal.

V. CHOIR TO GREAT

VI. SWELL TO GREAT

SWELL ORGAN 10 Stops, Tremulant and 1 Coupler.

26. OPEN DIAPASON*	8	Metal.
27. LIEBLICH GEDACT	8	Metal and Wood.
28. ECHO GAMBA	8	Metal.
29. VOIX CELESTE (ten. C)	8	Metal.
30. PRINCIPAL*	4	Metal.
31. MIXTURE	15,19, 22* -	Metal.

32. OBOE*	8	Metal.
VII. Tremulant.		
33. DOUBLE TRUMPET	16	Metal.
34. TRUMPET (harmonic trebles)	8	Metal.
35. CLARION (harmonic trebles)	4	Metal.
VIII. OCTAVE		

ACCESSORIES

Four combination pedals to the Pedal Organ.
Three combination pedals to the Choir Organ.
Five combination pedals to the Great Organ.
Reversible piston "Great to Pedal."
Reversible piston to "Swell to Great."
Reversible piston to "Swell to Tremulant."
Two balanced crescendo pedals to Choir and Swell organs.

WIND PRESSURES

Pedal fluework,	4 1/2′	reeds 10′
Choir,	4 1/2′	
Great fluework,	4 1/2′	reeds 10′
Swell fluework and oboe,	4′	reeds 7′
Action	10′	

The pedalboard to be radiating and concave, and each key to be faced with hard teak.

The drawstop jambs to be set at an angle of 45° to the keyboards, the keyboards and stop heads to have solid ivory fronts. The speaking stops to be lettered in black and the couplers in red. The couplers to be grouped with the speaking stops of the organs they augment. The whole of the mechanism is to be on our latest system of tubular pneumatic action, as in our organs in Durham, Gloucester, Oxford.

Appendix V: Harrison & Harrison 1931 Estimates.

Scheme II (Those ranks marked * are likely to have been reused from 'the old organ.')

PEDAL ORGAN, 6 Stops, 3 Couplers [CC-f1]

1. OPEN WOOD*	16	Wood.
2. SUB BASS*	16	Wood.
3. GEIGEN	16 (from No.10)	Metal.
4. OCTAVE WOOD	8 (18 from No.1)	Wood.
5. FLUTE 8	(18 from No.2)	Wood.
I CHOIR TO PEDAL		
II GREAT TO PEDAL		
III SWELL TO PEDAL		

CHOIR ORGAN 7 stops, 1 Coupler (in a swell-box)

6. VIOLA DA GAMBA*	8	Metal.
7. STOPPED DIAPASON*	8	Wood.
8. WALD FLUTE	4	Wood.
9. CLARINET*	8	Metal.
IV SWELL TO CHOIR.		

GREAT ORGAN. 12 Stops, 2 Couplers.

11. LARGE OPEN DIAPASON	8	Metal.
12. SMALL OPEN DIAPASON*	8	Wood and Metal.
13. GEIGEN	8	Metal.
14. CLARIBEL FLUTE*	8	Wood.
15. OCTAVE	4	Metal.
16. HARMONIC FLUTE*	4	Metal.
17. OCTAVE QUINT	2 2/3	Metal.
18. SUPER OCTAVE 2		
V. CHOIR TO GREAT		
VI. SWELL TO GREAT		

SWELL ORGAN 10 Stops, Termagant and 1 Coupler

19. OPEN DIAPASON*	8	Metal.
20. LIEBLICH GEDACT	8	Metal and Wood.
22. ECHO GAMBA	8	Metal.
22. VOIX CELESTE (ten. C)	8	Metal.
23. PRINCIPAL*	4	Metal.
24. MIXTURE	15,19, 22* -	Metal.
25. OBOE*	8	Metal.
VII. Tremulant.		
26. DOUBLE TRUMPET	16	Metal.
27. TRUMPET (harmonic trebles)	8	Metal.
VIII. OCTAVE		

ACCESSORIES

Three combination pedals to the Pedal Organ.
Two combination pedals to the Choir Organ.
Four combination pedals to the Great Organ.
Reversible piston "Great to Pedal."
Reversible piston to "Swell to Great."
Reversible piston to "Swell to Tremulant."
Two balanced crescendo pedals to Choir and Swell organs.

WIND PRESSURES

Pedal fluework,	4 1/2 ";	reeds 10".
Choir,	4 1/2 ".	
Great fluework,	4 1/2"	reeds 10".
Swell fluework and oboe ,	4"	reeds 7"
Action 7".		

The pedalboard to be radiating and concave, and each key to be faced with hard teak.

The drawstop jambs to be set at an angle of 45° to the keyboards, the keyboards and stop heads to have solid ivory fronts. The speaking stops to be lettered in black and the couplers in red. The couplers to be grouped with the speaking stops of the organs they augment. The whole of the mechanism is to be on our latest system of tubular pneumatic action, as in our organs in Durham, Gloucester, and Oxford.

The organ to contain four separate reservoirs, and with bellows panel containing valves is to be removable. The whole organ to be rebuilt from its foundations on a new main frame as a new instrument.

The best portions of the present organ to be carefully restored and preserved. The Pipework utilised again is to be thoroughly cleaned and restored, transposed where necessary, rescaled and revoiced with new pipes added in the bass. The organ is to be tuned to the new French pitch, i.e, $c^2 = 517$ vibrations at 60 degrees F.

£3,096-0-0 and the old organ.
1st March
The Revd. W.F. Wood,
The Vicarage,
CHIPPENHAM,
Wilts.

Appendix V1:

J.W.Walker's 1962 Estimate.

Letter to Canon Snow of 2nd November 1962:

The instrument contains some very fine material but we consider that the tonal quality is handicapped by poor regulation. The balance of power between bass and treble seems to us to be wrong, and thus as well as making alterations to the specification, such as remodelling of Mixtures and the Choir Organ, we have legislated for rescaling, tonal finishing and balancing of the various choruses. The console and the soundboard action work are, of course, very much worn and the wear on centres and moving parts makes the action rather slow and unresponsive to the touch. The soundboards also need completely overhauling and remaking as there are many leakages and 'runnings.'

The new action throughout would be electro-pneumatic of the most modern design and the console, which we understand it is proposed to detach, would be designed to harmonise with the furnishings of the Church and would be complete with a full complement of thumb and toe pistons adjustable by our latest improved type of selector switches nearly arranged under the Music Desk. The console draw-stops would be of a special and individual design whereby a slight toggle resistance has been incorporated, thus ensuring a clean and definite 'stop' and 'start' to the drawstop knob, when operated by hand or toe pistons...

CHIPPENHAM PARISH CHURCH, WILTS.

SPECIFICATION AND ESTIMATE FOR REBUILDING, MODERNISATION AND ELECTRICIFCATION OF ORGAN, INCORPORATING THE BEST OF THE OLD PIPEWORK AND OTHER MATERIAL

Compass of Manuals CC to C² 61 notes
Compass of Pedals CCC to G 32 notes

GREAT ORGAN

1. Double Diapason	Old	16ft.	61 pipes
2. Open Diapason No.1	Old	8ft.	"
3. Gemshorn	Old Keraulophon	8ft.	"
4. Clarabella	Old	8ft	"
5.Principal	Old	4ft.	"
6. Harmonic Flute	Old	4ft.	"
7. Twelfth	Old	2 2/3 ft.	"
8. Fifteenth	Old	2ft.	"
9. Fourniture (19-22-26)	Old remodelled	III rks.	183 pipes
10. Sesquialtera (12-17)	Old remodelled	II rks.	122 pipes
11. Trumpet	Old	8ft.	61 pipes
12. Clarion	Old	4ft. 61	"

SWELL ORGAN

13. Open Diapason	Old	8ft.	61 pipes
14. Stopped Diapason	Old	8ft.	"
15. Viola da Gamba	Old New Bass	8ft.	"
16. Voix Celeste TC	Old Choir Gamba	8ft.	49 pipes
17. Principal	Old	4ft.	61 pipes
18. Rohr Flute	New	4ft.	"
19. Fifteenth	Old	2ft.	"
20. Mixture (19-22-26-29)	Old, remodelled.	IV rks.	244 pipes
21. Contra Fagotto	Old Oboe, new bass.	16ft.	73 pipes
22. Cornopean	Old	8ft.	61 pipes
23. Oboe (from No.21)		8ft.	"
24. Clarion	Old	4ft.	"
Tremulant			

CHOIR ORGAN

25. Gedeckt	Old Stopped Diapason	8ft.	61 pipes
26. Principal	Old Gemshorn	4ft.	"
27. Flute	Old	4ft.	"
28. Nazard	New	2 2/3 ft.	"
29. Piccolo	Old	2ft	"
30. Tierce	New	1 3/5	"
31. Crumhorn	Old Clarinet	8ft.	"

PEDAL ORGAN

32. Open Wood	Old	16ft.	32 pipes
33. Open Diapason (From No.1)		16ft.	"
34. Bourdon	Old Stopped Diapason	16ft.	"
35. Lieblich Bourdon	(Old Swell)	16ft.	"
36. Quint (from No.35)		10 2/3 ft.	"
37. Principal Old Violincello, [sic] new top octave.		8 ft.	44 pipes
38. Bass Flute (from No.35)		8ft.	32 notes

39. Fifteenth (from No.37)		4 ft.	"
40. Octave Flute (from No.35)		4ft.	"
41. Mixture (19-22)	New	2 ranks	64 pipes
42. Trombone	Old New Top Octave	16ft.	44 "
43. Fagotto (From No. 21)		16ft.	32 notes
44. Trumpet (From No. 42)		8ft.	"
45. Oboe (From No. 21)		4ft.	"

COUPLERS
46. Choir to Pedal
47. Great to Pedal
48. Swell to Pedal
49. Swell to Great
50. Swell to Choir
51. Choir to Great
52. Swell Octave
53. Swell Sub-Octave
54. Swell Unison off
55. Great and Pedal Combinations Coupled.

ACCESSORIES
Five thumb pistons to Choir.
Five thumb pistons to Great.
Five thumb pistons to Swell.
Five toe piston to Pedal.
Five toe pistons to Swell (duplicating).
One reversible thumb piston for Great to Pedal.
One reversible toe piston for Great to Pedal.
One reversible thumb piston for Swell to Great.
One reversible thumb piston for Choir to Great.
One general cancel thumb piston.
Balanced Swell Pedal.

DETACHED CONSOLE
Fittings of Oak and contrasting hardwoods polished or suitably furnished

Keys of Thick Ivory with overhanging fronts. Ivories laid in one piece without a joint.

Draw-stop Knobs with ivory heads and shanks; engraving on knobs to be of a neat and legible character.

Stop Jambs placed at an angle.

Pedalboard radiating send concave, Royal College of Organists' standard; hardwood frame and notes.

Piston Combinations adjustable (from the console) by the "Walker" key-switch selector.

NOTES:

ADJUSTABLE PISTONS These are actuated by the "Walker" method of selector switches that has an advantage over the usual setting piston in that no memorisation is necessary when setting the combination.

INTERIOR CONSTRUCTION AND MECHANISM OF THE MOST APPROVED AND MODERN CHARACTER.

NEW ELECTRO-PNEUMATIC ACTION installed in place of the existing action; the mechanism designed to give instantaneous attack; prompt and crisp release and faultless repetition. All contacts of keys, relays, silver and non-corrosive alloys. Magnets to be of our latest design, having an extremely high resistance with consequent low-current consumption, thus eliminating deterioration of ` contact elements through sparking.

COUPLING MECHANISM to be all-electric of the most up-to-date and reliable design.

CABLES between console, organ couplers and soundboards to be of copper, plastic enamel or Polyvinyl Chloride (PVC).

SOUNDBOARDS opened up, the pallets taken out, stripped of old leather and completely recovered with the best quality sheepskins and felt; new plated steel springs and pull-down wires throughout.

NEW WIND CHESTS for Pedal and off notes to be of the latest and most modern design, constructed of the finest timber and materials, and designed to give ample speaking room for all pipework.

DRAWSTOP ACTIONS AT SOUNDBOARD END to be of the latest and most improved quick and silent in operation.

SWELL BOX overhauled and the interior lined with a hard sound reflective material. Shutters refelted, re-centred and refitted as necessary and made to be operated by a new elctro-pneumatic swell engine of our latest and most improved design.

BUILDING FRAME altered and re-made as necessary.

WIND RESERVOIRS overhauled and re-leathered where practicable and alternatively new reservoirs and wind regulator supplied to provide an ample and independent wind supply to the various departments; new roller pallet wind control throughout.

NEW WIND TRUNKING with some of the old incorporated.

NEWWIND BLOWING EQUIPMENT capable of delivering an ample supply if wind to the organ at the required pressure, with push-button switch for keyboard control.

SELENIUM-PLATE MAINS RECTIFIERS supplied to provide the necessary low-voltage current for the organ mechanism.

NEW PIPEWORK to be of the best description, plain and spotted metal of best quality, basses below tenor C of hard rolled Zinc with thick metal tips, lips and ears. Wood pipes of specially selected timber, all pipes adequately and liberally scaled.

OLD PIPEWORK thoroughly overhauled and cleaned; metal pipes rounded and repaired where necessary; those of wood to have all stoppers greased, re-packed and adjusted.

TINNED TUNING SLIDES supplied and fitted where required and practicable to open flue pipes.

REED STOPS entirely re-voiced, new tongues, wedges and springs inserted throughout, the shallots re-faced and burnished. Every pipe to receive careful and individual treatment on the voicing machine.

FLUE STOPS - Sundry Flue Stops removed from the organ and sent to the factory for complete re-voicing and the matching of new basses etc. to conform to the existing scheme as a whole.

PITCH to A = 440 and C = 523-3 at a temperature of 60^0 Fah.

ORGANIST'S BENCH of substantial construction.

CASEWORK AND PIPE FRONTAGE cleaned down and refurbished. The dummies on the West end of the case to be removed and a suitable grille fitted in their place. New panelling fitted in their place. New panelling fitted in the place vacated by the old console designed to match the existing casework.

SITUATION The organ to remain as at present but the internal lay-out redesigned to give better egress of tone.

The console to be detached - the final position of the console to be agreed...

WE UNDERTAKE to carry out the whole of the foregoing work.......FOR THE NET CASH SUM OF £8,190, 0s 0d.

****

Appendix VII

Rushworth & Dreaper's 1963 Estimate.
Rushworth & Dreaper Ltd., Great George Street, Liverpool 1
Dear Sir,
We are pleased to learn of the further interest in rebuilding the organ and recall our earlier negotiations during April 1961 when we submitted a detailed specification and estimate for carrying out similar work. During the interim period there have been a number of uplifts in wage rates throughout the trade, with a new Working Rules Agreement and we, regret, therefore, having to invoke the Validity of Estimate clause by reasons over which we have had no control.

As we understand the original scheme has been mislaid, we have taken the opportunity of retyping the estimate so that we might have the figures up to date, including the supplementary items which will further develop the reconstruction should further funds be available.

We cannot but emphasise the presence of woodworm in the construction of the organ and as this pest spreads into the mechanism if allowed to remain indefinitely, but we hope that finance will now allow of [sic] serious thought being given to the organ. Whilst opened up for close inspection, each section could be examined and we would advise a liberal spraying of a strong insecticide where practical to guard against deterioration after the organ has been re-assembled, That particular is, therefore, provided for in the estimate.

We would apologise for the delay in letting you have our current figures, due to illness of our technical staff...

Chas. Lythgoe.
Executive Director.

REVISED SPECIFICATION AND ESTIMATE TO REBUILD THREE MANUAL AND PEDAL PIPE ORGAN, WITH REMODELLED RECESSED DRAWSTOP CONSOLE, INCORPORATING ELECTRO-PNEUMATIC ACTION THOUGHOUT, PLUS TONAL REFINEMENTS.

Compass of Manuals CC - C 61 Notes (Console Only)

Compass of Pedals CCC - F 30 Notes

PEDAL ORGAN

1. Contra Bourdon	32ft.
2. Open Diapason	16ft.
3 .Stopped Diapason	16ft.
4. Violoncello	8ft.
5. Trombone	16ft.
I Choir to Pedal	
II Great to Pedal	
III Swell to Pedal	

CHOIR ORGAN

6. Dulciana	8ft.
7. Viol D'Gamba	8ft.
8. Stopped Diapason	8ft.
9. Gemshorn	4ft.
10. Flute	4ft.
11. Piccolo	2ft.
12. Clarinet	8ft.
IV Sub Octave	
V Unison Off	
VI Octave	
VII Swell to Choir	

GREAT ORGAN

13. Double Diapason	16ft.
14. Open Diapason No.1	8ft.
15. Open Diapason No.2	8ft.
16. Clarabella	8ft.
17. Principal	4ft.
18. Harmonic Flute	4ft.
19. Twelfth	2 2/3 ft.
20. Fifteenth	2ft.

21. Sesquialtera	III Rks.
22. Fourniture	II Rks.
23. Trumpet	8ft.
24. Clarion	4ft.

VIII Choir to Great
IX Swell to Great

SWELL ORGAN

25. Lieblich Bourdon	16ft.
26. Open Diapason	8ft.
27. Stopped Diapason	8ft.
28. Gamba	8ft.
29. Principal	4ft.
30. Fifteenth	2ft.
31. Mixture	IV Rks.
32. Cornopean	8ft.
33. Oboe	8ft.
34. Clarion	4ft.

X Tremulant
XI Sub Octave
XII Unison Off
XIII[Super] Octave

ACCESSORIES

Four Thumb Pistons to Choir Organ.
Six Thumb Pistons to Great Organ.
Six Thumb Pistons to Swell Organ.
Reversible Thumb Piston operating 'Choir to Pedal' coupler.
Reversible Thumb Piston operating 'Great to Pedal' coupler.
Reversible Thumb Piston operating 'Swell to Pedal' coupler.
Reversible Thumb Piston operating 'Swell to Great' coupler.
Reversible Thumb Piston operating 'Swell to Choir' coupler.
Six Toe Pistons to Pedal Organ.
Six Toe Pistons to Swell Organ, duplicating Thumb Pistons.
Reversible Toe Piston operating 'Great to Pedal' coupler.
Reversible Toe Piston operating 'Swell to Great' coupler.
Draws stop connecting 'Great and Pedal Pistons.'
Balanced Expression Pedal to Swell Organ.
Adjustable Switchboard for setting stop combinations placed in a convenient position in the console.

DETAILS OF CONSTRUCTION

GENERAL

The organ to be rebuilt on the present site; the recessed console to be remodelled with all electric action giving full of couplers and accessories, The oak panels of the console doors to be replaced by glass.

Preparatory general cleaning, the pipes to be removed from the soundboards and stored in a safe place adjacent to the instrument whilst work is in progress. After the pipes have been removed, all accumulated dirt to be extracted from the interior of the instrument by vacuum process.

CONSOLE

Keys The naturals to be covered with translucent material, the sharps to be of burnished ebony.

Drawstops The existing draw stop jambs to be refaced and new stop-knobs and solenoid actions fitted; ivory headedstop-knobs, with names engraved in capital letters; ebony stop stems to work in ivory and ebony bushings through the jambs.

Couplers to be grouped in the departments they augment and lettered in red,

Manual Pistons of ivory.

Pedal Board to be radiating and concave to the Royal College of Organists' scale.

The Balanced Swell Pedal to be re-covered with non-slip rubber and working centre lubricated.

Stool to be cleaned and given a coat of clear polish.
Adjustable Switchboard for setting stop combinations placed in a convenient position in console and protected by a lock from unauthorised interference.

MECHANISM

The "Rushworth" electric system to be employed for the entire mechanism to give immediate response and clean repetition of every touch of the player on key, pedal or stop.

Key, Pedal, Coupler and Relay contacts of silver wire, fixed in laminated sections. Magnets to have high resistance windings, impervious to residual magnetism; chest magnets fitted with detachable and adjustable caps.

Main cables and subsidiary cables to be fully protected and insulated by outer covering against atmospheric influence.

SOUNDBOARDS

The Choir and Swell soundboards to be dismantled and thoroughly overhauled, pallets to be re-covered best felt and sheepskin; the old leather of the 116 secondary motors to be cleaned off and re-covered with best quality sheepskin; new springs and connecting wires inserted and the working surfaces of tables, slides and upperboards re-fitted and polished with graphite.

The Great soundboard to be opened for inspection; the 58 secondary motors to be re-leathered, valves cleaned and bedded, springs re- set and lubricated. The working surfaces of tables and upper boards to be re-fitted and graphited; connecting wires to be adjusted to ensure correct movement of each pallet. The Manual auxiliaries to be overhauled, the 116 movements to be re-covered with best white sheepskin; valves bedded, springs re-set and each individual movement regulated to ensure instantaneous response.

The Pedal soundboards to be opened up for examination, tables, slides and upper boards polished with graphite; the old leather of the 60 secondary motor lifters to be cleaned and recovered with the best white sheepskin; pallets cleaned, new springs inserted and all movements adjusted for reliable service.

The existing changeover machines to the Pedal, Choir, Great and Swell to be dismantled and converted to electric introducing new magnets and auxiliary movements.

The Manual and Pedal stop actions to be taken to pieces; woodworm affected parts to be destroyed and replaced with new seasoned timber. The leather of the action motors to be cleaned off and each ribbed motor to be re-covered with best quality leather. New `electric to charge machines to be supplied and fitted - 5 Pedal stops and 29 Manual stops.

TREMULANT

A new Swell Tremulant to be supplied and fitted.

RESERVOIRS

Necessary repairs to the hinges and corners to be made with best white sheepskin and general leakages rectified. Control valves adjusted to give reservoirs the maximum rise.

ELECTRIC BLOWER

The electric motor and blower to be examined , bearings flushed out and replenished with clean oil. The whole plant cleaned of rust and surface dirt. No replacement parts are allowed for to the equipment and should such be considered advisable, the Church Authorities would be advised before incurring further expense.

RECTIFIER

A Selenium Rectifier to be installed supplying low voltage current for the action with full wave rectification and necessary smoothing.

WIND DUCTS

All wind ducts and conveyances to be examined, re-bedded and made air-tight at the terminals.

EXPRESSION BOX

The louvres to be refitted and felted to obtain the maximum diminuendo and adjustments made to secure freedom of movement. All centres on louvres and connecting rods to be lubricated and worn centres replaced. Louvres facings affected by woodworm to be replaced and all louvres given a treatment of insecticide.

BUILDING FRAME

The badly woodworm affected main frame rails supporting a main part of the organ to be removed and destroyed, and a new rail inserted of seasoned timber and ample thickness.

EXTERIOR CASEWORK

The exterior casework and front pipes to be cleaned.

WOODWORM

Replacements of parts of the organ damaged by woodworm, (other than mentioned under separate headings), are excluded from this estimate. The full extent of damage cannot be ascertained until the organ is dismantled and all parts opened up. The Church Authorities would be notified if there are any further replacements necessary, when additional cost could be determined. The woodwork of the organ to be given a liberal treatment with Rentokil insecticide as a precaution.

PIPEWORK

The speaking pipes to be thoroughly mopped and cleaned, repaired where necessary. dents in the bodies of metal pipes removed, and tuning slides fitted as required. Stoppers of wood pipes to be re-fitted and greased.

REVOICING

The following reed stops to be brought to the Factory for attention by our reed voicing specialist. A new reed tube to be supplied for the bass CCC note of the Pedal Trombone 16ft:

Pedal Trombone 16ft; Choir Clarinet 8ft; Great Trumpet 8ft; Great Clarion 4ft; Swell Cornopean 8ft;

Swell Oboe 8ft; Swell Clarion 4ft.

Brass reed shallots to be refaced and burnished and new tongues of specially-prepared, hard rolled brass fitted to entire register. New tuning springs and hard wood wedges fitted to each individual pipe.

All reed stops, as named, to be voiced to give the true character of the tone they represent and balanced to suit the specification of the organ and the acoustic properties of the building.

After revoicing, each pipe to be wrapped and carefully handled until replaced in the organ by a tone finisher and when in position regulated to produces the artistic standard associated with our work.

RE-ASSEMBLY

When re-assembled in their respective racks and speech adjusted to give the best possible tone, the of the various stops to be made even throughout the compass and the organ fine-tuned.

PITCH

The existing pitch to be retained,

MATERIALS AND WORKMANSHIP

Materials used in construction to be the best of their kind and the workmanship of the highest class.

INSURANCE

New parts of the organ to be insured by us during the course of reconstruction at our Factory and whilst in transit to the Church; responsibility for insuring the organ upon arrival at the building, whether in whole or part, to rest with the Church Authorities.

RE-ERECTION

Free access to the Church to be granted to our staff for the purpose of re-erection; also such light, power or heat as may be required and undisturbed quietness in the building during the tonal finishing of the organ.

COMPLETION

The organ to be finished in every detail and handed over in good playing condition to the Church Authorities.

ESTIMATE .... £4,480. - 0-.0.

Appendix VIII: Martin Goetze and Dominic Gwynn

'The organ was visited by Dominic Gwynn on August 1st 2003, in the company of the Vicar, Simon Tatton Brown, the director of music Graham Davis, and Christopher Kent.

The estimate is for a new organ, using the restored case, the surviving Brice Seede pipework and Gray & Davison pipework where suitable, reconstructing elements of the Seede organ where appropriate, and making new parts in the classical English style. The organ is to be relocated on new west end gallery, with space for choir and musicians.

We would be delighted to be asked to carry out this project. It has all the elements which excite us: it is based around surviving parts of a well-made Georgian organ, of a kind well able to demonstrate its suitability for the wide range of music in today's parish church; it is to be reconstructed in its original position, in a large church with a good acoustic. The organ will be part of musical life in an active parish church, where it will be used by fine musicians and as an inspiration for new ones.

One of our most successful organs has been the almost identical project to St. Helen's Bishopsgate in the City of London. It too had the nucleus of an excellent Georgian organ buried in an increasingly rebuilt organ, moved to the east end of the church. The following list gives the amount of 1752 material remaining and the amount of material to be incorporated into the new organ, the notes taken almost entirely from Christopher Kent's article in BIOS Journal vol. 14.

GREAT ORGAN (11 stops)

Open Diapason	8' C-c#1 or f1 in the front, some 1752 inside pipes in Great and Swell
Stop Diapason	8' some of the bass pipes survive in the Great, 28 on the Choir
Principal	4' in halves, 39 1752 pipes survive
Flute	4' none survive, unless in the Great or Choir Stop Diapasons.
Twelfth	2 2/3' 21 1752 survive
Fifteenth	2' 12 1752 pipes survive
Sesquialtera	III some 1752 pipes survive

Furniture	III some 1752 pipes survive
Cornet V treble	
Trumpet	8' about 30 1752 pipes, revoiced but with original resonators, blocks and shallots
Cremona	8'

CHOIR ORGAN (4 stops)

Stop Diapason	8' as above
Principal	4' "
Flute	4' "
Cremona	8' "

SWELL ORGAN (8 stops)

Open Diapason	8' bass half 1879, treble half 1752?
Stop Diapason	8' treble half of rank 1752, stopped metal
Gamba	8' 1879
Principal	4' bass half 1879, treble half 1752
Fifteenth	2' "
Cornet	II "
Hautboy	8' 1879 revoiced
Trumpet	8' "

PEDAL ORGAN (4 stops)

Open Wood	16' about 18 pipes ca. 1850
Bourdon	16' using 1879 pipes
Principal	8' "
Trombone	16' using 1879 pipes restored to original condition.

This will be a new organ using Seede's case and pipework, and a few elements of the 1879 Gray & Davison organ. Although the Swell and Pedal would not have been part of Seede's organ, it would appeal to us to work within the history of the organ as far as possible.

The console details (and indeed the rest of the organ to be made new would follow Seede's practice as far as possible, as provided by models at Powderham Castle and Lulworth Castle, unless there are reasons not to. The wind chest would be based on that at St. Helen's Bishopsgate.

The key and stop action would be all new, but made of natural materials in the traditional English fashion . The advantage is that such actions, for which we are choosing appropriate materials and in making and keeping the organ in an appropriate environment, will last for as long as it is possible for an organ mechanism to last.

The stop action will be modified partly to accommodate a mechanical combination action, so that the most commonly used registrations are available, in a fashion similar to that applied in [the] Gray & Davison organ with the prospect of agonising and expenditure 30 years down the line (or less; the life expectancy of electric organs gets shorter `with each new generation).

The wind will be supplied by a German fan blower (Aug. Laukhoff), twice the price and twice as good as the English ones. It will be regulated by a large horizontal bellows of the kind that Gray and Davison would have supplied in 1879. The result is in our opinion more musical than the wind supplied by more modern systems.

CASEWORK

The case is a wonderful piece of joinery and in the organ world an exceptional survival. As Christopher Kent says, that makes its treatment an area for consideration on its own. That is our view as well. Although we are woodworkers, and have considerable experience in restoring historic cases, I often feel that we are doing work better done by experts in the field. In this case, the main problem is the treatment of fragile surfaces which have been covered with layers of varnish.

SUGGESTIONS

The Vicar asked for answers to some pertinent questions which will be aimed at advocates of this organ scheme. Some of these have been addressed by Ian Bell's judicious report, and others answered by Christopher Kent, but I hope it helps to provide an answer or two here.

1. The first relates to the reduction in the size of the organ from 46 speaking stops to 27. The first thing to point out is that the gradual enlargement of the last century of Gray & Davison's organ of 1879, which had 34 stops is directly responsible for the organ's increasing lack of reliability, and for the increasing frequency of repairs and rebuilds. This is partly because the organ was provided first with pneumatic and then electro pneumatic key and stop actions. These types of action make it easier to enlarge the organ, but each addition makes the organ more complicated and more haphazard. They are also less reliable and durable than traditionally made and designed mechanical key action.

2. The second thing to point out is that a smaller organ is perfectly adequate for this church. It would be a suitable size for the space, although organists always require more stops for the ever-increasing repertoire of music, in practice most music is realisable on organ of quite modest size. The larger the organ becomes, the more limited the purpose of each new stop.

Appendix IX William Drake

Great Organ, GG/AA - a3, 62 notes

Open Diapason	8
Stopped Diapason	8
Principal (in halves)	4
Twelfth	2 2/3
Fifteenth	2
Sesquialtera	17.19.22 III
Furniture	II suggest III ranks (as originally?)
Cornet middle c to d3	V possibly IV ranks instead
Trumpet (in halves)	8
Cremona	8

Choir Organ, GG/AA - a3 62 notes

Stopped Diapason	8 from Great
Flute	4 from Great
Principal	4 treble independent
Cremona	8 from Great

Swell Organ, CC-a3, 58 notes

Open Diapason	8 bottom octave grooved into S.D. with 'helpers'
Stopped Diapason	8
Gamba	8 bottom octave grooved into S.D.
Principal	4
Fifteenth	2
Cornet	II
Hautboy	8
Trumpet	8

Pedal Organ, CC-f1, 30 notes

Open Wood	16
Bourdon	8
Principal	8
Trombone	16

Couplers

Great to Pedal, Swell to Pedal, Swell to Great, Swell to Choir.
Pull-down levers for GG/AA BBb/BB
Four mechanical composition pedals to Great & Pedal and Swell.
Tremulant
Straight and concave pedalboard.

Appendix X Peter Collins Ltd.
Great

Open Diapason	8 Seede & new
Stopped Diapason	8 Seede & new
Principal Treble	4 Seede & new
Principal Bass	4 Seede & new
Flute	4 new, stopt
Twelfth	2 2/3 Seede & new
Fifteenth	2 Seede & new
Sesquialtera	III Seede & new
Furniture	II Seede & new
Cornet	V mid c, new
Trumpet Treble	8 new
Trumpet Bass	8 new

Choir

Stopped Diapason	8 transmission from Gt.
Principal	4 transmission from Gt.
Flute	4 transmission from Gt.
Cremona	8 new

Swell

Open Diapason	8 old & new
Stopped Diapason	8 Seede & new
Gamba	8 new
Principal	4 Gray & Davison
Fifteenth	2 Gray & Davison

Cornet II Gray & Davison from IV
Trumpet 8 Gray & Davidson revoiced
Hautboy 8 Gray & Davison revoiced

Pedal

Open Wood	16	present
Bourdon	16	present
Principal	8	present
Bass Flute	8	derivation from Open Wood 16
Fifteenth	4	derivation from Principal 8
Trombone	16	present
Trumpet	8	derivation from Trombone 16

Couplers
Swell to Pedal, Great to Pedal, Choir to Pedal, Swell to Great, Swell to Choir

Accessories
4 combination pedals to Great & Pedal
4 combination pedals to Swell

Compass
Great & Choir GG/AA - a3 62notes
Swell CC - a 3   58 notes
Four toe studs to couple GG, AA, AA#, BB
Pedal CC - f1   30 notes

Mechanical action to manuals, pedals and stops. Position of instrument: the new organ to be placed within the existing

1752 Seede case and organ be placed upon a new west gallery.

Appendix XI.

Analysis of Seede organ case finishes by Catherine Hassell, 2013.

St. Andrew's Church, Chippenham.

The organ case was built in 1752 by Brice Seede. A sample of carving, with brown varnish layers, was sent for examination by Dr. Christopher Kent.

Examination The piece was examined under low magnification, and then several fragments of wood with the brown coating on them, were mounted in cold-setting polyester resin, to be cut as cross-sections. The sections were viewed at high magnification in halogen and in UV fluorescent light, and the layers compared. Material from the brown layers was dispersed on a glass slide, and the pigments were identified by polarised light microscopy at magnification x1000.

RESULTS

The front of the carved leaf had just one coat of varnish on it. This varnish was tinted a dark brown by the addition of finely ground particles of iron oxide and carbon black pigment [see Sample 1, p.3].

The edges and the back of the leaf have a much thicker coating, and the cross-sections shows at least two layers, both tinted with brown and black pigment particles [see Sample 2, p.3]. The final layer in the samples taken from the edges is so heavily pigmented that it is completely opaque, and is therefore more of a paint than a varnish.

It is puzzling that there are more coatings at the back and sides of the carving, than on the front. Perhaps the front was stripped, or partially stripped, at some point. This would explain why there are so few layers, when normally one would expect to find a build-up of many coats of varnish.

Comment
There is no way of dating the layers, as the brown and black pigments are ones which have been in continuous use since earliest times, but the coatings on this carving are not what one normally finds on eighteenth-century church oak paneling.

The most commonly found treatment is for the hardwood to have been either left unvarnished, or given a very thin coat of oil varnish. Over the years, further coats of varnish tend to get added, and in the nineteenth century these tended to be varnishes based on natural resins. Resin varnishes start out clear, but turn brown with age.

On this particular carving the varnishes were all deliberately tinted a dark brown. This is unusual, and suggests that the coatings on this particular piece of carving could be late finishes.

C. Hassall, Paint Analysis Report no.B175
5, Patshull Road, London NW5 2JX   September 2013

SAMPLE 1
Showing just one
layer of varnish on
the wood

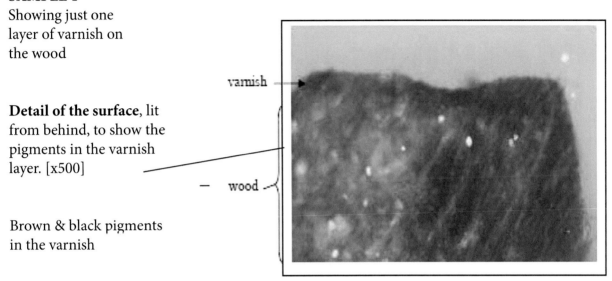

Detail of the surface, lit
from behind, to show the
pigments in the varnish
layer. [x500]

varnish

wood

Brown & black pigments
in the varnish

SAMPLE 2

From edge of leaf [x200]

This had more than one layer.

Top opaque layer containing a lot
of black & brown pigment

Brown varnish, less heavily
pigmented than the top one, [like
the one in Sample 1]
[split in sample]

Wood

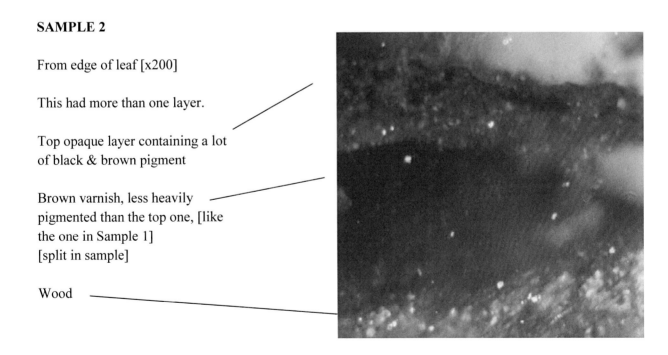

THE PARISH CHURCH OF ST ANDREW, CHIPPENHAM
WITH ST NICHOLAS, TYTHERTON LUCAS
VICAR: THE REVEREND SIMON TATTON-BROWN, THE VICARAGE, 54A ST MARY STREET, CHIPPENHAM, WILTS.
SN15 3JW
www.standrewschippenham.2day.ws

Churchwarden:
Ros Harford
101 Studley Hill
Studley
Calne Wilts
SN11 9NL
Tel: 01249 812190
email: rosharf@supanet.com

Churchwarden:
Margaret Harrison
9 Riverside Drive
Chippenham Wilts
SN15 3NU
Tel: 01249 652148
email: margaret9rd@tiscali.co.uk

16th March 2005

Dear Parishioner

The St. Andrew's Project

Since the St. Andrew's Project was launched to the congregation last May, with a Civic Launch following in December 2004, it has become clear to the Project Director, Vicar, Churchwardens and the Project Campaign Committee that many members of St. Andrew's congregation feel unhappy and concerned with various aspects of the Project.

We are all agreed that the problems of the organ, toilet facilities, kitchen facilities and the heating need to be tackled. However, great reservations remain. The fundraising effort can only continue against a background where there full confidence in the Project.

In order to receive the benefit of the feelings and thoughts of the whole congregation, an **Open meeting is to be held on Tuesday 12th April 2005 at 7.30 pm in the Church**. To assist with the planning of the meeting, it would be most helpful if you would complete the tear-off slip.

The meeting will be chaired by independent Chairman, Mr Keith Cocking, and will be so arranged as to provide every opportunity to express your views concerning all aspects of the Project. Your opinions will be carefully considered and documented and will be taken into account when drawing up future plans for the Project.

If you are unable to attend the meeting, then please put your thoughts or questions in writing, anonymously so if you wish, address them to the Churchwardens, and put them through the Church Office letterbox. It is our most earnest wish that all members of our congregation make every effort to attend this important meeting – if transport is a problem, then please let the Churchwardens know and arrangements can be made.

Yours sincerely

Ros Harford & Margaret Harrison
Churchwardens

To the Churchwardens, St Andrew's Church Office

Name ....
I *will / will not be able to attend the Project Open Meeting to be held in Church on Tuesday 12th April 2005. *delete as appropriate

Appendix XII: Letter of 2005 presaging the meeting which terminated the St. Andrew's Project.

PROJECT OPEN MEETING – TUESDAY 12TH APRIL, 2005 – 7.30 p.m.

Introduction:

Arrangements for the structure of the Open Meeting have yet to be finalised but it is hoped that a number of Groups (each with a facilitator) will be set up to discuss particular issues. A plenary session will then be held to hear the outcome from each Group.

Scope of existing Project:

Detailed plans and costings for the St. Andrew's Project were drawn up in April 2002. The main elements consist of:

1) Restoration and relocation of the organ to its pre-1878 position on a purpose built gallery at the West end of the Church.
2) Construction of an entrance Narthex (or porch) beneath the gallery to accommodate a toilet facility and to provide a quiet area for young children and their families.
3) Re-positioning the War Memorial Screen to form the front of the Narthex.
4) Provision of 2 toilets in the space vacated by the organ (one to be fully accessible), plus a storage area for chairs.
5) Kitchen facilities at the West end of the North aisle, to be boxed in and invisible when not in use.
6) Installation of a new heating system and relocation of radiators round the base of the nave columns.

An outline of the above elements is shown on the attached drawing.

Group facilitators will describe the *benefits* and *estimated costs* for each of these elements during the meeting. The facilitators will also describe the *consequences* of not proceeding with any or all of the elements.

Points to bear in mind:

1) The Disability Discrimination Act came into force in October 2004. We are statutorily obliged to make every effort to provide fully accessible toilet facilities in the Church building.
2) The Council for the Care of Churches reported in February 2005 that they supported the main elements of the Project with two important reservations. Firstly, the Council strongly advised that the War-Memorial Screen is left in its present position and that an entirely new organ gallery is provided in 18th Century style. Secondly, the placing of heating radiators round the base of the nave columns is not recommended since the column bases are attractively carved and are one of the only decorative features of the medieval building to survive.

Before the meeting please take time to think carefully about the following:

1. Which elements of the Project are essential and which are not?

2. Fund-raising. What can we afford? How can we raise the money, bearing in mind the other repairs to the church building recommended in the Quinquennial Survey of 2004?

3. What alternative suggestions can you offer, if the present Project is beyond our means?

4. Do you wish to be more involved with the Project? If so how would you like to contribute?

MARCH 2005

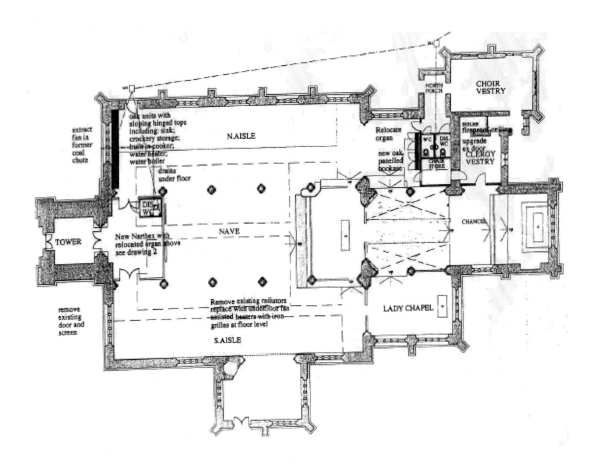

The ill-fated plan of the 'St Andrew's Project' by the church's former architect Christopher Romain.

Appendix XIII

Analyses of the metal compositions of Brice and Richard Seede's Organ Pipes.

During 1981 two of the Great Organ high register mixture pipes of the instrument were replaced by Percy Daniel & Co. on account of the collapse of their mouths and languids after successive pitch changes and the damage to their bodies by cone tuning. The late Managing Director of the firm, Christopher Manners, made these available to the author at The University Reading Department of Music for analyses by the Department of Chemistry via the process of Atomic Absorption Spectroscopy. Two samples were tested from each pipe produced the following results:

Sample One: Pb - 74.10 %   Sample Two: Pb - 76.75%
              Sn - 23.87%   Sn - 20.76%
              Sb - 0.04%   Sb - 0.04%
              Total - 98.01%   Total 97.55%

Four years later during the historically informed restoration of Richard Seede's 1785 organ in Lulworth Castle Chapel by the late William Drake following pre- restoration research by the author working under the aegis of B.I.O.S. for Sir Joseph Weld some untidily discarded shards of pipe metal, stemming from a pitch change, were found at the base of the instrument and were subjected to the similar laboratory tests at Reading.

Sample One: Pb - 74.77 %   Sample Two: Pb - 77. 22 %
             Sn - 25.32 %   Sn - 24.19 %
             Sb - 0.04 %   Sb - 0.08 %
             Total - 100.22 %   Total - 101-49 %

The author is most indebted to Professor David Rice and Dr. Allen Munday for their work.

Appendix XIV:
International letters in support of the failed St. Andrew's Project of 2005.

From Dr.Pierre Dubois, Sorbonne, Paris IV.

Dear Dr. Kent,

I thank you for sending me your brief about the organ at St. Andrew's Parish Church in Chippenham. You know my long-lasting attachment to historically-informed projects of restoration or reconstruction. I am delighted to see that your proposal for the organ of Chippenham Parish Church takes its history and original characteristics into account.

The fact of returning the organ to a West Gallery, where Seede had originally erected it (as organ-builders would do at the time), is the first essential decision and I cannot but approve it wholeheartedly, as I do the fact that the preservation and restoration of the fine case should be another priority. I am equally satisfied with the decision to build "an organ with fully mechanical action throughout with a tonal design based on the original Georgian Classical scheme". I do not know the instrument well enough to judge whether the quantity of material from the 1879 Gray and Davison organ justifies incorporating some aspects of the High Victorian period. There is no doubt, however, that the two most sensible alternatives are either the reconstruction of the Seede organ, or that of "a musically acceptable and reasonably versatile instrument incorporating and respecting significant elements of its history". The drawback – by today's standards – of the absence of pedals in a "pure" Seede-based instrument will of course be avoided if one opts, as you suggest, for a versatile "classical" instrument incorporating some aspects of its nineteenth-century evolution. Finally, the composition seems to meet all the requirements for such an instrument in its original surrounding.

I am personally convinced that your proposal, which was, I understand, duly approved by the Association of Independent Organ Advisers and by the Organs Advisory Committee of the Council for the Care of Churches, is an excellent one both in terms of preservation of what survives of the historic instrument and in terms of the present-day use and future fame of this organ.

With my best regards,

Pierre Dubois.

Sorbonne, Paris IV.

∗∗∗

Margaret Phillips, Royal College of Music, London.

Dear Chris,

I was very excited to hear about the proposal to rebuild the organ of Chippenham Parish Church. Though I have not visited the church, the historic case is renowned in organ circles and it would be a wonderful achievement to restore it to its original position on the west gallery. The organ would regain its integrity both as a musical instrument and as a magnificent piece of furniture, and would thereby greatly enhance the worship of the church. I have recently made recordings in Germany on two early 19th century instruments which have been restored in an appropriate style on west galleries, and the musicians and congregations of both churches are delighted with the musical and liturgical possibilities which have been created. I very much hope that your project will come to fruition, and wish you every success.

Margaret Phillips

Professor of Organ, Royal College of Music, London

13 March 2005

***

From Dr. John Watson, Colonial Williamsburg, U.S.A.

Dear Christopher,

It was good to hear from you, and to see the important work you are doing with Chippenham Parish Church.

I hope the congregation knows how much the organ's long presence in the church serves as a musical and physical link among generations of their kin. Layers of technological, musical, and aesthetic alteration, can erode such a connection. I hope the church will take this new opportunity to celebrate their own auspicious heritage. As a lover of organ music, I truly hope the 1752 organ can be restored and preserved in a way that honours those who saw fit to provide such a significant organ for the church.

Sincerely,

John R. Watson Conservator of Instruments, Colonial Williamsburg Foundation, Williamsburg, Virginia.

***

From: Dr. Paul Peeters: Director, Göteborg University Organ Art Center (GOArt)

Göteborg, 16 March 2005

Dear Dr. Kent!

It is with great interest that I have read your plan to relocate and rebuild the organ of St. Andrew's Parish Church Chippenham. Given the importance of both instrument and case, I most strongly support your plan, which not only takes the history of the instrument into account (and rescues as well as incorporates parts that are worthwhile to be preserved), but also will create a highly qualitative and versatile instrument that can function well in worship and as solo or ensemble instrument.

Dr. Paul Peeters.

From: John Maidment, University of Melbourne.

Dear Chris,

Thank you for your message. I am more than delighted to offer support for the proposals you have prepared for the organ at St Andrew's Parish Church, Chippenham.

I would make the following comments:

1. The organ will sound immeasurably superior in its rear gallery location and take advantage of a greatly improved acoustical situation. Its sounds will clearly project to all parts of the building and not be stifled by masonry, as is the case at the moment. The quality of sound will be superior too, and although the organ is smaller, it will effectively sound larger and more impressive owing to the location. Clearly, additions were made in the past to counter less than satisfactory transmission of sound to the nave.

2. The tonal scheme respects all of the earlier material and incorporates it in an instrument that has overriding stylistic integrity. All components would combine effectively - the sum total of the parts would be greater than the actual resources. A return to mechanical action additionally will promise an instrument of great longevity, unlike its predecessor, and encourage performers to give of their best. Location of all musicians in the reconstructed rear gallery will offer direct and superior support to the congregation assembled below.

3. Preservation of the distinctive and rare organ case in its original location will offer the church a strong focal point - there will be an excellent match between sight and sound. The church will have an instrument that is a considerable source of pride.

I trust that the congregation will take up your proposal with considerable enthusiasm. It will offer an instrument of enormous artistic distinction that will offer valuable service for generations. Hoping that these comments are of value.

Kind regards,
John Maidment, O.A.M.
Chairman, Organ Historical Trust of Australia.

From: Dr. Göran Grahn, Stockholm.

I think your project in Chippenham seems very good indeed, and I do approve fully of your idea. I hope you will be able to convince the PCC. My position is Curator at the Nydahl Collection in Stockholm and also organ historian and organ consultant and organist at the Anglican Church of St. Peter & St. Sigfrid, Stockholm.

Appendix XV

Checklist of compositions by James Morris Coombs I.

Published by Preston, London, unless otherwise stated.

1790   Te Deum and Jubilate as Performed at Salisbury Cathedral.
1800   A March [...] Inscribed to the Armed Association of Chippenham.
1805   To her I love oh waft that sigh.
1805   Rural Content: a pastoral glee.
1806   We meet no more, oh think on me.
1806   Haste let the roses, a favourite glee.
1810   Mary's Grave.
1810   Eight Canzonets with Accompaniment for the Pianoforte
1815   Grand Chorus (arr. from C.H. Graun's Te Deum).
1819   Coombs's Divine Amusement. Second edition 1825.
1820   Oh! Henry! With doubts like these?
n.d.   The Banks of the Dee, a favourite air [...] arranged as a rondo for pianoforte
        Colliford, Rolf & Barrow.
n.l.   Agnus Dei (incomplete).

In manuscript:

RCM, MS 157
Te Deum and Jubilate in G for 4 voices and figured bass.
6 Chants: 1 in Eb; 2 in E; 3 in D; 5 in C minor; 6 in D. 8ff.
The sixth chant has a note in Coombs's hand, to J.W.Windsor: 'I send you this chant merely as a curiosity,
I have no idea that it will ever be sung.'

RCM, MS 158
'I like to behold the bright stream', song with pianoforte accompaniment. 2ff.

RCM, MS 159
Sonata in C for Pianoforte, 'Presented to Mr. Windsor by the composer.'

RCM, MS 674
'Organ Book./St. Margaret's Chapel/Bath/J.W. Windsor organist 1798'.
psalm chants:
No.23
No.41 Psalm 9
No.57 Psalm 4
No. 63 Psalm 119
No.93 Psalm Tune 4 voc.

RCM, MS 674
A further organ volume: 'This book was bought at the expense of the Proprietors of St. Margarett's
[sic] Chapel'
contains the following chants by J.M. Coombs:
No.24 Psalm 105
No.49 Psalm 13

MSS of 'Blessed is the man' by [George] Combes (Gloucester Cathedral Library).
MSS of 'Out of the deep' by [George] Combes (Oxford Bodleian Library MS Mus. 424-425)

Henry Baker's Book 1814 (manuscript in private ownership) contains the following verse anthems by [George?] Combs for SATB strings, and organ:

No. 18 'Lord I have loved the habitation of thy house', Psalm 26, p.96
No.19 'Seek the Lord while he may be found'. p.102.

Arrangement of Benjamin Cooke's 'How sleep the brave' to words by William Lisle Bowles (1815) n.l.

Appendix XVI

Checklist of compositions by James Morris Coombs II.

Published (by J. Alfred Novello, London):

1830   You told me once my smile had power No.41 Psalm 9
1835   Musical Sketches for the Pianoforte No.1
1830   Compilation: A Collection of Sacred Music, containing Psalm chants by James Morris Coombs I & II.

In manuscript:

f1.   W. Croft 'The souls of the righteous', composed for the funeral of Queen Anne
f.14   J. Blow, P. Humfrey, and W Turner 'I will always give thanks'. 'The Club Anthem.'
f.18   P. Humfrey 'By the waters of Babylon.'
f.23   P. Humfrey 'Lord teach us to number our days'.

Christopher Kent grew up in Chippenham and first attended this church in the late 1950s and a decade later began organ studies there with John Tomlins. He read music at the University of Manchester, studied organ and conducting at the Royal Manchester College of Music, and Musicology at King's College London. In 1973 he received the Hilda Margaret Watts Prize for the M.Mus. examination. He gained the F.R.C.O. diploma in 1975, and received a Louise Dyer Award for research into British Music from the editorial committee of *Musica Britannica* in 1976.

After completing a Ph.D. on Elgar's sketches he continued organ and harpsichord studies with Susi Jeans and Gustav Leonhardt prior to joining the Department of Music at the University of Reading in 1980 where he established an influential postgraduate course in Organ Historiography. From 1986-96 he served as Hon. Secretary of The British Institute of Organ Studies. In 2002 following a bereavement, he retired from his position at Reading University as acting Head of Department, to devote more time to research, writing, and performing.

His main publications include *An Elgar Research Guide*, contributions to the *Cambridge Guide to Elgar*, the *Cambridge Musical Instrument Guide to the Organ*, *The New Grove Dictionary of Music and Musicians*, *Die Musik in Geschichte und Gegenwart* and *The New Dictionary of National Biography* and *The Canterbury Dictionary of Hymnology*.' He has served as an organ adviser to the Dioceses of Oxford and Salisbury and served for two quinquennia as a member of the Organ Advisory Committee of the Archbishop's Council for Church Buildings.

He is a member of the Association of Independent Organ Advisers, a Liveryman of the Worshipful Company of Musicians and a Fellow of the Society of Antiquaries of London. He has performed widely in Britain, Croatia, France, Italy, Portugal, Slovakia and the U.S.A. Recent papers at musicological conferences include the 2006 Handelfest in Halle and the 2008 and 2009 Oxford Symposiums of the British Institute of Organ Studies. He was honorary organist at the chapel of St Nicholas, Tytherton Lucas 1973-2013, and occasionally deputy or assistant St. Andrew's since 1968. Latterly, this has been dependent on the vagaries of propitious parochial politics. His recordings include the organs of the Stiftkirche, Klosterneuberg, Austria (Freundt 1632) and the *Walpurgiskirche*, Grossengottern, Germany (Trost 1716)[179] which was inspirational for instrument in Bowood House chapel (Collins 2002)[180] for which he was the consultant and is currently Honorary Organist. Locally, he has served as consultant for the restoration of an organ by William Allen of ca.1810 for the church of St. Martin's Bremhill, Wiltshire. In 2010 he received an award from the British Academy to enlarge a second edition of his Elgar Research Guide, to include a thematic catalogue. This was published in 2013 when he was also elected to the Trustee Council and Awards Committee of the Royal College of Organists. In 2015 he received the C. B. Oldman Award of the International Association of Music Libraries, Archives and Documentation Centres, for the second edition of his 'Elgar Thematic Catalogue and Research Guide.'

181

The author at the console of The Temple Church, London prior to a recital in March 2015 (Susan Kent).

REFERENCES

1   British Organ Archive Notebooks of The Revd. Andrew Freeman.

2   W.S.A. ref: 891/2-3.

3   *John Aubrey, Wiltshire Topographical Collections,* A.D. 1659-1670 collected and enlarged by John Edward Jackson (The Wiltshire Archaeological and Natural History Society, Devizes, 1862) p.68.

4   John Jeremiah Daniell, *The History of Chippenham,* Houlson, Bath & Chippenham, 1894. C Chippenham, 1894. p.141

5   *ibid.* p.143

6   *ibid.* p.145

7   B.O.A: Freeman *op cit.*

8   *ibid.* I p.6

9   Stephen Bicknell, *The History of the English Organ*, Cambridge, 1996, pp.23-25.

10   Dominic Gwynn 'Two pre-reformation English soundboards *The Organ Yearbook XXVI* (1996).

11   W.S.A. ref: 1769/20

12   W.S.A. ref: 2664/8

13   W.S.A. ref: 730/97

14   W.S.A. Keary Stokes & White deposit, ref: 415/6

15   Sperling Note Books vol. III: B.L. Loan 79.9/3 p.102.

16   *ibid.* p.103

17   *Daily Journal* 5th June 1729.

18   *Salisbury Journal* 13th September 1743.

19   WSA Goldney Deposit, ref: 473/400

20   Charles Avison 'Essay on Musical Expression with Related writings by William Hayes and Charles Avison', ed. Pierre Dubois, Ashgate, 2004, p.101.

21   *ibid.* p.34

22   *ibid.* p.101

23   William Lisle Bowles, *The Parochial History of Bremhill,* London: John Murray, p.174.

24   Pierre Dubois, 'The Organ and its Music Vindicated' - a study of 'Music Sermons' in eighteenth- century England. JBIOS 31 (2007) pp.40-64.

25   John Eden, *Church Music: a Sermon preached at the Opening of the New Organ in the Parish Church of St. Nicholas, Bristol* (Bristol), p.15.

26   Information kindly supplied by Anne Willis.

27   W.S.A. ref: 811/27 f.51.

28   *ibid.*

29   *ibid.* p.64.

30   *The Chippenham Chronicle,* September 26th 1879.

31   *The Salisbury Journal*, December 4th 1752.

32   John Dix , 'The Life of Thomas Chatterton' Hamilton Adams and Co., London, 1837.

33   Christopher Kent, 'An Introduction to Brice and Richard Seede: Organ Builders of Bristol'. JBIOS 5 (1981) 83-97.

34   GRO ref: P86a CW 2/1

35   *The Gloucester Journal,* 26th April 1748.

36   G.R.O. ref: P86a CW 2/1

37   Letter to the author: 2nd March 2013.

38   *The Freeman-Edmonds Directory of British Organ Builders,* Positif Press Oxford, 2003, vol. 3, p.621.

39   *ibid.*

40   *ibid.*

41   Denise M. Neary, 'Organ-building in seventeenth and eighteenth Dublin, and its English connection.' JBIOS 21 (1997) p.24.

42   W.S.A. ref: 1312/32 f.141: Church Account book 1733-81.

43   *ibid.*

44   W.S.A. ref: 811/54

45   Christopher Kent, 'An Introduction to Brice and Richard Seede: Organ Builders of Bristol' *J.B.I.O.S. 5* (1981) p.89.

46   W.S.A. ref: 811/27 f.67v.

47   W.H.M. ref: MSS 224 & 225 *passim.*

48   *ibid.*

49   *Bath Gazette 4th October 1805.*

50   B.L. ref: 1026.f.1. (6.)

51   *The Salisbury and Winchester Journal,* 20th August, 1815.

52   Benjamin Cooke, *A collection of glees catches and canons : for three, four, five and six voices,*William Thomson, London, [1775]

53   Collection of Guy Oldham.

54   Two anthems ascribed to James Morris Coombs by Marshall (1840) and Foster (1901) in the library of Gloucester Cathedral: 'Blessed is the man that feareth the Lord' and 'Out of the deep' are also likely to be by George Combes.

55   Facsimile edition of Russell's *Complete Voluntaries,* ed. Gillian Ward Russell, 1991.

56   Unpublished lecture to the Corsham Historical Society by the author, 2013.

57   *op.cit.*

58   R.I.S.M. U.K on line.

59   L.B.L. Harleian MS 7338 ff.96v.- 98. Author's transcription.

60   *The Salisbury and Winchester Journal,* March 13th 1820.

61   James D. Brown and Stephen S. Stratton, *British Musical Biography,* Birmingham 1897, p. 99

62   Glasgow University Library, Euing Collection ref: h.d.85/49

63   *Biographie universelle des musiciens et bibliographe générale de la musique,* Paris (1835-1844).

64   *Musik Lexicon* (1882).

65   2nd Edition, ed. Fuller Maitland, Macmillan, London 1902, vol. 1 p.597.

66   W.S.H.C. ref: 811/64.

67   *Ibid.*

68   Nicholas Thistlethwaite, 'Source materials from the early 19th century.' *JBIOS,* vol. 1 pp.75-100.

69   Nicholas Thistlethwaite, *The Making of the Victorian Organ,* Cambridge, 1990, p.99.

70   W.H.M. ref: D77/3.

71   *q.v.*

72   *Harmonicon,* 1824, vol.2 part 1.

73   For a complete list of compositions and arrangements by Coombs (father and son) see Christopher Kent, 'Music of Rural Byway and Rotten Borough.' *Music in the British Provinces 1690-1914,* ed. Cowgill & Holman (Ashgate 2007), pp.179-181.

74   *Keene's Bath Journal* 19th August 1822.

75   *The Bath Chronicle,* 15 May 1816.

76   R.C.M. MS. 1,067.

77   R.C.M. MS.158.

78   B.L. Add. MS. 65489 ff. 198-109v. The author is most grateful to Fiona Palmer of the National University of Ireland, Maynooth, for bringing this to his attention.

79   *The Ladies' Monthly Museum or polite Repository* April 1816 p.25.

80   The son of the second marriage of the First Marquess to Lady Louisa Fitzpatrick. Known as Lord Henry Petty from 1784 to 1809, he was one of the most distinguished Whig politicians of the first half of the 19th century: Chancellor of the Exchequer 1806 to 1807; Home Secretary 1827 to 1828;
      Lord President of the Council 1830 to 1834; 1835 to 1841 and 1846 to 1852; Minister without Portfolio 1852 to 1858; twice declined to become Prime Minister and refused the offer of a Dukedom in 1857.

81   Bowood Archive.

82   Diary of C.R.Cockerill R.I.B.A. collection: V.&A. Museum, ref: CC/9/3.

83   *Ibid*. ref: D=CC/9/4.

84   *Ibid*. 8th July 1823.

85   David Watkin, *The Life and Work of C.R.Cockerill, Zwemmer, London 1974*. Plate 157.

86   Cockerill's case and possibly some pipework were reused for the new instrument by J.M.Holdich commissioned in November 1843.

87   Mary Berry, Journals vol.III p.460, *Extracts of the Journals and Correspondence of Miss Berry, from the Year.*
      1783 to 1852 (3 volumes;), ed. by Theresa Lewis, Longmans, Green, London, 1865.

88   National Pipe Organ Register, ref: ST976705.

89   Peter Collins & Christopher Kent 'A New Trost Organ for Bowood Chapel Wiltshire', *Journal of the Institute of British Organ Building* , vol. 6, (2006) 48-53.

90   q.v. recording by author on PRCD 855.

91   W.H.M. ref: 1982.3294.

92   W.A.M. vol. XLVII p.185.

93   Lambeth Palace Library ref: CBS (ref: 3846).

94   W.H.M. ref: 873/395.

95   J.Lee Osborne, Chippenham an ancient Saxon town, its surroundings and associations. *ter, Wilts. and Gloucestershire Standard, 1921. ibid.*

96   W.H.C. ref: 137/87

97   W.H.M. ref: MS 2332

98   W.H.M. ref: 137/87

99   *ibid.*

100   Rodney Matthews, *op.cit.* vol. I pp.85-88.

101   *The Lyra Ecclesiatica*, ed. Revd. Joshua Fawcett, preface by W.H.Havergal, Rivington, London, 1844, pp.63-67 .

102   R.C.M. ref: C118/1.

103   L.B.L. ref: G.502.(7.)

104   Vol. 6. 15th May 1854 p.65.

105   *The Musical Times* June 1st 1859, p.67.

106   Nicholas Temperley, *The Music of the English Parish Church*, vol.1, Cambridge, 1979, 272, 287, 298.

107   Devizes and Wiltshire Gazette 20.3.1913.

108   Courtesy of Paul Fortune.

109   J. Lee-Osborn. *Chippenham: an Ancient Saxon Town…*, Cirencester, 1921.

110   *The Chippenham Chronicle*, September 26th, 1879.

111   *ibid.*

112   *Western Daily Press* 9th July1880.

113   W.S.A. ref: 811/97

114   As a point of clarification this Parish remained in the Diocese of Salisbury until 1836 when it passed to the Diocese of Gloucester and Bristol, the present Diocese of Bristol (following a medieval precedent) was created in 1897.

115   *Devizes and Wiltshire Gazette,* 7th May 1868, p.3. col.4.

116   *Hymns Ancient & Modern,* 1st ed., Novello, London, 1861.

117   *Devizes and Wiltshire Gazette,* 8th January 1874.

118   *Bath Express & North Wilts Guardian,* 20th March 1875.

119   *Wiltshire Independent,* April 12th 1866.

120   W.H.C. ref: 1789/20

121   *ibid.*

122   19th January 1878.

123   B.B.C. Radio 3 talk by Dame Gillian Weir on reopening the restored organ of Gloucester Cathedral, at the 1971 Three Choirs Festival.

124   *The Chippenham Chronicle,* Saturday 19th January 1870, p.2.

125   Peter Horton, 'Edward John Hopkins: an organist and choirmaster re-examined (II)' *The R.C.O. Journal,* vol. 4 (new series) 2010, p.29.

126   B.I.O.S. website.

127   B.O.A. Gray & Davison Factory Book ref. Organ No. 10412.

128   *Western Daily Press,* 9th July 1880.

129   *The Salisbury Journal,* March 27th, 1852.

130   *The Church Builder* 1867, pp. 164-167.

131   *The Musical Times,* vol. 30, 1st January 1874.

132   *The Church Builder* 1873 pp. 68-71.

133   J.R.M.A. vol. viii, 1881-2.

134   William Gaskell, *Wiltshire Leaders,* Queenhithe, London. [1906] p.25.

135   Author's collection.

136   W.S.A. ref: 811/98

137   W.H.M. ref: 1760/18

138   W.S.A. ref: 2512/170/46

139   *North Wiltshire Guardian,* January 3rd, 1908.

140   *The Wiltshire Telegraph,* January 4th, 1908.

141   W.S.A. ref: 811.98

142   W.S.A. ref: 118.40

143   Durham County Record Office ref: D/Ha 104 pp.346-351.

144   *ibid.* D/Ha 104 pp.110-111.

145   WHM ref: 1760/18 typescript transcription by Harry Ross.

146   *Devizes and Wiltshire Gazette,* April 10th 1924, p.6.

147   WSA ref: 2568/18

148   WSA ref: 2568/14

149   Examples of his work can be seen at Derry Hill (originally by Holdich) where a second manual was added with barely enough space for tuning access; at Kington St. Michael (1912) third manual with inadequate casework was added and plus a Hope-Jones style Diapason Phonon. Similarly at Grittleton 1 (1910) the tonal alterations also included impositions at variance with an instrument of 1856.
       He added a third manual to the Clark/Sweetland organ of St. Paul's Chippenham. In the early 1990s this instrument was unwisely disposed of to a Slovenian organ builder who attempted to restyle it in a new church at Celle. The Clark case was destroyed in an attempt to emulate the style of Holtkamp's caseless organs. The repairs to the pneumatic action were a failure to the extent that when the author visited the instrument in 1994 it was unplayable.

150   Bicknell *op.cit.* p. 208ff.

151   Details supplied by kind permission of Harrison & Harrison Ltd.

152   W.S.A. ref: 2568/14.

153 W.SA. ref: 2568/16.

154 *Radio Times*, March 28th 1952, p.16.

155 W.S.A. ref: 2568/17.

156 *ibid.*

157 Batsford, London, 1963, p.95.

158 W.S.A. ref. 3714/ 25

159 W.S.A. ref: 2512/170/46.

160 W.S.A. ref: 2512/170/46.

161 *q.v.* St. Anne's Limehouse, London, and Usk Parish Church, Monmouthshire.

162 W.S.A. ref: 3908/2.

163 W.S.A. ref: 3908/3.

164 W.S.A. ref: 3714/15.

165 W.S.A. Paraphrase of letter yet to be accessioned.

166 W.S.A. ref: 3908/3

167 *ibid.*

168 W.H.C. ref: 3908/4/i.

169 *JBIOS* vol.17, 1993, 4-17.

170 W.S.A. ref: 2512/170/46.

171 Copy supplied to the present writer by Ian Bell.

172 *ibid.* p.4

173 Christopher Kent, *The Organ of St. Andrew's Parish Church Chippenham, first edition published b by the Vicar and Churchwardens, Chippenham*, 1976; Second edition 1984, p.23.

174 *op.cit.* p.18.

175 Martin Freke, 'Anglican Church Organists 1950 - 1999: A Study of Challenges to Musical, spiritual and Cultural Orthodoxies.' Unpublished Ph.D. Thesis University of the West of England, 2005.

176 Christopher Kent, 'Brice Seede of Bristol: some further findings.' JBIOS 17 1993, 4-17.

171 Wednesday 8th May 2013; this was certainly the finest possible reflection of the aesthetic and historical foundations of this instrument in the 'Music Unlimited' lunchtime recitals presented by 'The Friends of St. Andrews' which had contributed to successively to the Roof, Tower and Organ Funds since 2005 only to fall prey to the vacuous agendas and petty politics of two church officials during an interregnum.

172 APSCD 220.

173 PRCD 85.5.

INDEX